CW00962450

These 22 short stories span over a
Helena and her family, forming a m
four generations. The family saga i
mother from Galicia to Prague whe
husband. Helena's parents emigrat.
and then return after the war hoping to build a better society.
History repeats itself. Helena's idyllic childhood in Czechoslovakia
is cut short by the Soviet invasion and her own emigration to
England. These very personal stories are loosely based on real
events and encompass the trials and joys of marriage,
motherhood, divorce, friendships and a scientific career. They
begin with the engagement of Helena's 13-year-old grandmother
in Galicia and end with a description of the funeral of Helena's
cyclist friend in London.

*Helena Zelená (a pen name) was born in London, grew up in
Prague and returned to London again as an adult. She worked as
a lecturer and a cell biologist until her retirement. Helena lives in
London and has two sons and three grandchildren whose
paintings are shown on the book cover.*

First Printing, 2016

ISBN-13: 978-1532854507
ISBN-10: 1532854501

1

Long Life in Short Stories

Helena   Zelená

For my family and my friends

CONTENTS

WHAT MY MOTHER TOLD ME

1910-1930

My mother's first memory was from 1914. At the start of the 1st World War, her family decided to leave their village and move to Vienna to escape the war and the pogroms. Their property was loaded onto twelve wagons. My mother sat in one of them with a maid, who suddenly farted loud and clear. That shocked the little girl more than the marauding Cossacks.

My mother Amalia (Malka) was born in 1910 in a small village of Wojutycze near the Galician capital Lvov; part of the Austro-Hungarian Empire at the time. Her parents were Frida and Abraham Szuster, both orthodox Jews. Frida (Frimcze) was the only daughter of Michael and Gita Dresner; her father Michael (Mechle) was a farm manager. Abraham Szuster was one of four children; he had two brothers and one sister. Like his father-in-law, he too was a farm manager.

Abraham Szuster: Malka's father

Frida got engaged to Abraham in 1891 when she was only 13 and he 16 years old. One day, Frida was playing ball with other children on the street when her mother Gita called her.

"Get dressed, Frimcze, 'shadchen' (the matchmaker) has arrived!"

Frida cried, she wanted to continue playing but she did as she was told. Abraham and Frida were married a couple of years later and over time had five children, though only three survived. Malka was the youngest child. Her brother Josef was fourteen years older and her sister Ginka four years older than her.

Frida and Josef, Malka's mother and brother

During their escape to Vienna, the family stopped in Slovakia and lived there for some time in a rented house. It was there that the Cossacks attacked them. One of the soldiers grabbed Abraham's beard and waved his sword about. Abraham and Frida begged for mercy. Josef, who was then 18, took his little sister Malka in his arms, jumped out of a window and ran. The agitation gave him a nosebleed which covered Malka in blood. When they returned home Frida thought they were wounded and fainted in dismay. She was pregnant at the time and lost the baby. My mother used to have nightmares about this episode for many years.

Only two of the twelve initial wagons were left when the family finally reached Vienna. They rented a little house in

Mödling, just south of the city. Malka went to school there for five years. They led a traditional Jewish life, celebrating Jewish holidays and making sure their children learned Hebrew. My mother remembered how, on Sukkot holidays, her father together with a Mr. Lipmann would sing religious songs in a special hut called 'sukkah'.

After the war, their home country Galicia became part of the West Ukrainian People's Republic for a short and turbulent time. Eventually it came under Polish control. My grandfather Abraham was the first one of the family to return home. He rented a farm "Roguzhno" near a small town called Sambora (or Sambir). My grandmother Frida followed later with their daughters.

Ginka and Malka, went to school in Sambora. They lived there during school terms with their granny Gita (Frida's mother). Malka remembered the time in Sambora as a very happy period; she adored her granny. On winter Saturdays, a big horse-drawn sleigh would come from Roguzhno to fetch the girls and take them back home for the weekends. In summer it would be a carriage.

Roguzhno farm was not doing too well and so in 1920 the whole family, including granny Gita, moved to Stryj, a small town about 70 km south of the Galician capital Lvov. Malka's mother Frida had inherited a house there from her father Michael. A four room family apartment was on the upper floor, a clothes shop was downstairs and six small apartments were let to tenants. My mother continued her education in Stryj. The beloved granny Gita lived with the family for further five years; she died in Stryj in 1925 and was buried in Sambora.

Malka's brother Josef had remained in Vienna to study Hebrew and Arabic as he wanted to be a rabbi. When he had finished his studies, he was offered a rabbi position in the USA, but Frida was doggedly against it: "So weit!" she said. So far! In the end, Josef became a teacher at a grammar school in Vilno (then in Poland, now capital of Lithuania). It was the first ever Hebrew grammar school in Vilno. When in 1935 Frida died, Josef emigrated to Palestine. There he met and married Regina, an ornithologist, and altered his name to the Hebrew Josef Shiloh, meaning tranquil, peaceful, serene.

Tranquil, peaceful, serene? My mother, as a teenager, was none of these. When she was fourteen years old, she joined 'Hashomer Hatzair' (The Youth Guard), a left wing Zionist organisation. These young people were looking for a way to keep their identity without the constraints of the Orthodox Jewish life. They studied Marx and other Russian revolutionaries and, influenced by the ideas of Theodor Herzl, they dreamed of creating a just society. Malka stopped believing in God and eating Kosher.

Around 1927, she wanted to take part in 'Haschara', agricultural work organised by the Hashomer Hatzair organisation. Such activity was aimed to prepare young people for life in a kibbutz. But Malka was not allowed to go to Haschara. "You should concentrate on finishing your grammar school!" her mother told her. Malka was actually locked at home in order to prevent her from running away. After long debates, she was finally allowed to go because it was a special occasion: the 23rd anniversary of Herzl's death. Malka travelled with her best friend, a fellow student Hela Goldmark. They worked on a farm for a whole month. Her first time away from home, Malka found the work – making

10

and baling hay - very hard. She missed her family terribly, sending such heart-breaking letters back home that her parents felt obliged to send her an occasional food parcel.

Malka (on the right) partying ~1926

Malka finished the grammar school in Stryj with distinction. She wanted to study medicine but was unable to do so in Poland because of the "Numerus Clausus," a law restricting the proportion of Jewish students. Instead, she was offered a place at the Faculty of Philosophy at the University of Lvov. Malka decided she would give it a try. However, she felt intimidated by the antisemitic atmosphere there and soon left.

Her other option was to study medicine abroad. She would then be able to come back to Poland and arrange to have her diploma recognized. She resolved to go to Prague, Czechoslovakia. She stayed in Stryj for another year working as a teacher to save as much money for her future studies as she could. During this time she was still with Hashomer Hatzair while

11

her best friend, Hela Goldmark, had already joined the communists. The two friends used to meet at night in a cemetery; there they secretly read The Communist Manifesto and discussed a better tomorrow. Hela also wished to study medicine but was penniless. Malka offered help: she paid the journey to Prague for both of them. The two friends left Stryj together in 1930.

Brother Josef was a great help to Malka. He supported her both financially and morally. My mother always spoke of him with a great affection. It must have been hard for her to be separated from him for some 25 years. Josef emigrated to Palestine in 1935. After the chaos of the war and after the oppressive totalitarian years in Czechoslovakia, Malka and Josef were finally reunited in 1960 when, during the so called 'thaw', my uncle Josef and his wife Regina arrived in Prague.

Josef, Regina and Malka, Prague 1960

I was too young to appreciate how much this reunion meant to my mother. I did note, however, that there was a whole new dimension to my mother's personality. These hidden qualities also became apparent when her old friend Hela, or Dr. Hela Grotkowska as she was later called, appeared in Prague. To my amazement, mother spoke fluent Polish to Josef or Hela, changing

12

into a different, giggly, sparkling and excited person, speaking in a shrill tone.

Hela Grotkowska always insisted on inviting all members of the family to come to Warsaw and stay with her.

"When will you come? I would so much like you to visit!"

Travelling out from the socialist Czechoslovakia was very difficult; an official invitation was needed. Therefore Hela's offers were very tempting. After I had got married to Paul, aged not quite nineteen, we decided to spend our honeymoon in Warsaw. I remember Hela as a little old lady, although she must have been only about 55 at the time. Whenever we admired anything in her Warsaw apartment, she would say "Take it, take it!" She was obviously 'downsizing'.

In June 2011, my sister, my Japanese sister-in-law and I agreed on a joint visit to Malka's country: to Lvov, Sambora and Stryj, now in Western Ukraine. We met in Krakow, Poland, where we acted as tourists: admired the castle Wawel, listened to the trumpeter playing an ancient tune from St Mary's church and indulged in 'serniky', the best ever cheese cakes. But there was a bizarre side to the town: we saw adverts such as "Tour Bus to Auschwitz and Wieliczka Salt Mine! - Enjoy our Special Offer! - Hundred Euros only!" In Kazimierz, Jewish Quarter, there were shops full of cute little wooden Jews and the cemetery contained walls constructed from broken Jewish graves. Odd, but at least the Jewish past of that city was acknowledged.

Not so in Ukraine. We took a sleeper train from Krakow to Lvov. The journey to Old Sambora required two other trains. We would have never found the old Jewish cemetery where my great grandmother Gita is buried without the help of a book by Ruth

13

Ellen Gruber: 'National Geographic Jewish Heritage Travel: A Guide to Eastern Europe' (thank you, Ruth). The cemetery was founded in the 16th century. Its renovation in 2001 was funded by a U.S. survivor from Sambora. When we got there ten years later, it was already completely overgrown. We could hardly find it behind the stone wall at the edge of a wood. The three of us staggered through high grass to admire the beautiful ancient gravestones and to contemplate the eeriness of the place. Afterwards, two local boys helped us to find what was left of the synagogue. Ironically, the building was situated in Khmelnytsky Street, a street named after the Cossack who in the 17th century led the Ukrainian uprising against the Poles and who was responsible for massacres of the Jews.

Jewish cemetery in Sambora

In Stryj, we found my mother's grammar school quite easily. A statue of Stepan Bandera stands proudly in front of it. He was the controversial leader of the right wing Ukrainian nationalist movement. On the grammar school's wall, a plaque with Bandera's bust remembers his attendance. Other statues,

14

monuments and plaques commemorate the gruesome history of the town during the war. Victims of bolshevism, victims of fascism. Atrocities were committed both under the Soviet (1939-1941) and the German (1941-1945) occupation.

Ginka, Malka's sister– around 1935

It was fortunate that my grandmother Frida died before the war. My grandfather Abraham was also lucky. During a blitzkrieg in 1940 he and my aunt Ginka, together with the tenants, were hiding in the cellar of their house. A baby was hungry and wanted milk so Grandfather Abraham went upstairs to get it. He was killed instantly by a bomb that hit the house. My aunt Ginka's story, however, was gruesome. In the first year of the German occupation, she wrote a letter to Malka's parents in law who then lived in the Protectorate of Bohemia and Moravia. In it she complained about how difficult life was for her. The letter was censored by the German occupiers. A soldier arrived at Ginka's door; she was pulled out by her hair and shot in the courtyard. Still, her fate was perhaps much better than that of thousands of others who were later massacred in the Stryj ghetto, in the nearby forests and in the death camps.

In 2011, we couldn't find a single acknowledgement of the fact that Stryj Jews, nearly 40% of the town's population were also victims of the war. I asked a young lady in the 'Museum of the Soviet Totalitarianism' about this. She was annoyed.

"We have enough trouble finding money for our own people's memorials!"

Holobutow forest near Stryj where Jews were murdered

THE SUNSHINE AND THE GATHERING CLOUDS OF THE 1930S: MALKA AND ERNEST

1930-1939

My mother Malka came to Prague in 1930 in order to study medicine. She came from Galicia where she was unable to study because of the law called "Numerus Clausus," which aimed to limit the number of Jewish students at Polish universities. She had financial support from her parents in Stryj and also from her older brother who at the time worked as a teacher in Vilnius (in today's Lithuania). Malka in turn supported her friend Hela from these funds, so the two girls had to live very frugally. They shared a small rented room and were sustained by one sausage and one egg per day, per person. Eventually, Hela received a grant and their life became easier.

When she was in the second year of her studies, Malka got to know my father Ernest, her fellow student. My father used to say he was bewitched by Malka's hazel doe eyes. Things progressed rapidly and in 1933 the two rented a place together in Prague - Nusle. Malka knew that her family would strongly disapprove of her 'living in sin' and did her best to avoid being seen together with Ernest. However, her parents and her brother found out – probably reported on by some fellow students from Vilnius; letters full of opprobrium followed.

Malka was becoming increasingly radical and not only in her private life. She joined the 'Kostufra' organization (**Ko**munisticka **Stu**dentska **Fra**kce, Communist Student Fraction) and wanted to change the world. Initially, Ernest kept back from all this. However, in the 1930s the tension at the German University of Prague was high. This was due to the presence of numerous right wing students, particularly those from the border areas. In neighbouring Germany, Hitler had quickly risen to power after the financial crisis of 1929; one of his strategies was the agitation of the German minorities along the Czechoslovak borders. Thus, my father eventually joined Kostufra as well.

Malka ~ 1930

To disturb a meeting of fascist sympathizers, Ernest took part in an antifascist demonstration. He was sentenced to two weeks imprisonment for disorderly behaviour. Since his exams were imminent, he appealed and the sentence was delayed until after his graduation. The latter took place on the 23rd of June 1936 and it was the first occasion for Malka to meet Ernest's parents. A week later Malka and Ernest got married. She wore a Humphrey Bogart style overcoat with a wide black belt and a matching black hat pushed to one side, a black leather envelope clutch handbag under her right arm, a bunch of roses in her hand. He put on a stripy black suit, white shirt with a very wide collar and wore round black-rimmed glasses à la John Lennon. His curly black hair was most probably controlled by some kind of brilliantine. On their wedding photo they look as if they just stepped out from a film noir.

July 1ˢᵗ 1936 Malka and Ernest's wedding

Instead of the honeymoon, Ernest was obliged to sit his two weeks in the Pankrác Jail. Ernest's parents were kept under the impression that all was as it should be and the happy couple were enjoying their honeymoon. Malka boarded the train, the 'Sázava River Pacific', alone and kept sending matrimonial postcards to her new parents in law.

"Having a wonderful time, you would love it here!"

One from Týnec, another from Čerčany and the last one from Mníšek. This story became an often repeated family yarn: "How Ernest had spent his honeymoon in jail".

My father Ernest was born in Ústí nad Labem (Aussig an der Elbe) in 1910, the middle one of three children. At that time, Ustí was still a part of Austria-Hungary, but after the 1ˢᵗ World War it belonged to the recently formed Czechoslovakia. The town, together with some areas along the Czech borders called the Sudetenland, was mainly inhabited by ethnic Germans. Until 1848 most Jews of the Austro-Hungarian Empire were not allowed to live in larger cities so it was only after that year that the Jewish

19

community of Ústí nad Labem began to develop. In the 1930s it consisted of about 360 families.

Anna and Josef, my grandparents

My grandparents Joseph and Anna, came from small villages: Joseph from Smolotely near Příbram (south-west of Prague) and Anna from Vraňany near Mělnik (north of Prague). My grandfather's family had been established in the Příbram region for at least four generations (since mid 18th century), initially in a village called Zbenice. The family had made minor moves but always in that area. Joseph had four brothers and four sisters and they all were born in that region. Grandfather Joseph's generation was the first to move further away and into larger cities.

None of the nine siblings survived the holocaust and thus, typically for my generation, I have never met any of my grandparents, great aunts or great uncles. Perhaps because the memories would have been too painful, my father talked very little about his family and childhood. I remember just a few of his

20

stories and the rest comes from whatever of relevance I could find online, in old documents, in books or from old friends and relatives. There are photos of my grandfather Joseph as a soldier in the Austro-Hungarian uniform, but alas no stories from his army days survived. He was said to be a bit melancholy and it was apparently my grandmother Anna, a kind and practical woman, who, in Ústí nad Labem, took care of a small shop selling ready-to-wear clothing.

Josef is 2nd on the right, standing row (~1915)

Anna was the oldest of five children. Her two sisters, Kamila and Rosa, also had shops in the nearby towns: Kamilla in Teplice and Rosa in Děčín. The three sisters liked to meet and discuss business together. Anna's two brothers were Rudolph and Erwin, both successful businessmen. Rudolf lived in nearby Litoměřice and Erwin in Prague. It was a close family. My father remembered the frequent visits of his aunties and uncles. He recalled how his mother Anna, my grandmother, used to make wonderful doughnuts and, leaning out of the window, she would call her neighbours to come and taste. Again, none of the five siblings of my grandmother's generation survived the holocaust.

The three sisters: Anna, Kamilla, Rosa (~1930)

Anna and Joseph had three children. My father had an older sister Trudi about who my mother said -in confidence - that she was a bit of a neurotic. That's all I know about her – but on the photo I have of her she looks quite self-possessed. On the other hand, the younger brother Pavel, my uncle, was a very jolly chap, football was his passion. My mother very much appreciated his tactfulness: once in the student days he visited Ernest in Prague and saw Malka hiding in bed under the cover. He just laughed and joked about it and never told anybody.

Ernest's first language and his education were German, but he also spoke fluent Czech. He studied at the German Realschule in Ústí until 1930 and then, after his Abitur, at the German Medical School in Prague. He loved both German and Czech literature, his favourites were Goethe, Heine, Kafka, Vančura and Čapek. As a teenager my father was a keen traveller. I found his passport, issued in 1926 when he was just 16 years old, the very same one which he used in 1939, when emigrating to

England. That old passport photo caused him a lot of trouble since by then he was already 29 years old! His first journey, however, was for pleasure: he travelled to Italy in 1926 and then again in 1928 and in 1933. It was a country of his dreams. Always, even in his late years, Ernest was trying to learn Italian. At every mention of anything Italian his eyes would lit up and he would sigh, "Oh bella Italia!"

Trudi, Ernest and Pavel (about 1920)

Between 1936 and 1938, my mother got to know Ernest's family well. There is a photo of her posing coyly in her swimsuit in front of a summery Lido pool. Uncle Pavel stands on her right in some sort of pyjama bottoms, while grandfather Joseph, in voluminous swimming trunks that are partially covered by a dressing gown, stands on her left. Life must have been pleasant then; exciting new jobs for the two young doctors, numerous family gatherings and many visits to the Prague 'Liberated Theatre' where they were still able to laugh at and make fun of the rise of Hitler in Germany.

Pavel, Malka and Josef

Judging from my father's passport, there must have been at least two occasions (1935 and 1937) when he visited Malka's family in Stryj, in Galicia. Perhaps it was he who took the picture of Malka and her sister Ginka sitting on a wooden balcony of a cozy "Apteka Sezonowa" (Seasonal Apothecary). What did Ernest think of Malka's family? What did they think of him? My father liked to joke about his visit to Stryj: with an ironical, meaningful glance at my mother he would proclaim: "Stryj – a pearl in the midst of Lesser Poland towns!" It was some kind of touristy waffle that he picked up on these journeys to Stryj. Perhaps that amused look of his still reflected the surprise he must have felt when he arrived, coming from the thriving industrial town of Ústí to the sleepy backwater of Galician Stryj.

Malka with her sister Ginka

In Ústí, relationships between the Germans, the Czechs and the Jews were friendly. So friendly, my father recalled, that sometimes – for example after an exciting football match – the agitated gang would smash a couple of Jewish windows.

"That taught you a lesson!" they would say laughing it off the next day and life went on as usual.

Ernest's parents lived in a modest house on Bĕlehradská Street, running their shop and enthusiastically supporting the Czechoslovak Social Democratic Party. Its German-speaking representative was Leopold Pölzl, twice voted as a mayor of Ústí by both the Czechs and the Germans. He was much admired by my grandparents.

However, in May 1938, Pölzl lost to a candidate of the Sudeten German Party (SdP). The aim of the SdP was to achieve autonomy for the German minority in Czechoslovakia and to push for the annexation of the border area (Sudetenland) with Germany. With mighty support from Hitler SdP succeeded. In September 1938 at a conference in Munich an agreement was negotiated without any Czechoslovak representatives: a pact was signed that permitted the Nazi Germany's annexation of Czechoslovakia's Sudetenland. Thus Ústí was now incorporated into the German Reich. The picture of the British Prime Minister Neville Chamberlain waving a piece of useless paper that was meant to bring "peace for our time" is well known.

Neville Chamberlain shakes hands with Adolf Hitler

That was the end of the good life. Leopold Pölzl was attacked by a gang of SdP members, beaten and imprisoned. The Nazis burnt down the Ústí synagogue. By that time, most Jews and many Czechs had left Ústí for places inside the truncated Czechoslovakia: my grandparents had moved to Prague. They were very worried about the situation but didn't want to leave the country.

"We have our pensions here; we are Czechs!"

Although they could have obtained help with their emigration from the fellow Social Democrats, they refused. However, their advice to Ernest and Malka was "Go."

At that time, my father worked as a secondary care doctor at a hospital in Vysoká nad Jizerou; mother was an assistant doctor at the Infectious Diseases Department in Prague Bulovka

26

Hospital. The anti-German feelings were high after the Munich debacle. Since both Malka and Ernest studied at the German University in Prague and Ernest had German schooling in Ústí, they were – ironically - suspected to be loyal Germans and lost their jobs.

On the 15th of March 1939 Hitler occupied Prague and the rest of the country. The already reduced Czechoslovakia was now split in two parts: Nazis controlled the 'Protectorate of Bohemia and Moravia' and Slovakia became a nominally independent fascist state. For my parents, getting out of the country became a necessity. My mother told me the story of their emigration.

Like many others, they were running around various embassies trying to get visas so that they could leave. Tram conductors, familiar with the situation, shouted the names of the appropriate embassies at tram stops:

"Englishmen out! Chinamen out!"

At the Gestapo Office on the Na Perštýně Street there were huge queues for travel permits. Malka and Ernest had been standing there since four o'clock in the morning one day at the end of March. It was the last day when the permits were still being issued. Finally, at about 11 o'clock, a Gestapo man came out of the building.

"Juden heraus!" he shouted. Jews out!

"What shall we do?" Malka and Ernest hesitated.

"Don't worry!" Some Polish people, who were just in front of them in the queue, reassured them. "This doesn't apply to you, only to the Jews." Malka and Ernest obviously did not fit the image for these Poles.

"Let's just stay here and see what happens," Malka decided and so eventually they got inside the office and presented their passports.

"When was your husband born?" A typical, blue-eyed and blond Gestapo officer asked Malka.

"July 17th 1910". My mother confused the date by one day.

"Ha ha, ha, your hubby wouldn't be very pleased if he got his presents one day late!!" The amused Gestapo man laughed and my parents got their travel permits stamped.

A colleague told them they were selling train tickets for England at the Wilson's Station (today "Hlavní Nádraží"). My father was troubled since they still didn't have the English visas, only their passports valid for all European countries except USSR.

"We can't afford to lose any time!" Malka said and bought the tickets anyhow. She also bought two warm blankets for the journey.

EXILE AND RETURN

1939-1946

The day of my parents' departure from Prague was March 30th 1939. Ernest's parents, Anna and Joseph, and sister Trudi came to the station to see them off. My father was still troubled about the lack of visas. He considered delaying the journey to make sure everything was in order. As they discussed these matters, a Jewish man overheard them.

"Do you have valid passports?" he asked.

"Yes."

"Do you have the Gestapo Permits, die Bewilligungen?"

"Yes."

"And you are still thinking about it? Are you mad? You are very lucky! What about me? I am getting onto the train with no Gestapo permission, no visa, with nothing, nothing at all! There is no time to waste!"

15th March 1939: occupation of Czechoslovakia

My parents got aboard and the train left the station. My mother was in tears; to calm herself down she started to walk around the train.

"Malka, Malka!" she heard someone calling. It was Kurt, Ernest's cousin. He was accompanied by his father Fritz. Uncle Fritz was married to my grandfather Joseph's sister, Marie.

"What a coincidence! How did you manage to get here?" Malka was delighted to have their company.

Fritz and Kurt explained they had paid 20 000 crowns to get their Gestapo Permits. They had planned this journey for some time and Fritz had already sent several machines from his electrical factory in Liberec (Reichenberg) for repairs in Belgium. He wanted to get them out of the country to have something to start with. They wanted to prepare the ground in London so that the rest of their family could come later to join them: Kurt's mother Marie together with her daughter Katherine and Katherine's family. As it turned out, March 30th 1939 was the last time that Kurt and Fritz saw their family and that Ernest and Malka saw theirs.

My mother remembered every detail of their train journey, especially the trouble they had at the Dutch border, in Bentheim. Gestapo men collected all the passports and brought them back later, all except my father's. His name was called. He was told to get out.

"Oh please, please, let him go!" my mother was sick with anxiety.

The problem was that Ernest's passport was too old - the photo inside it was taken when he was sixteen.

"Das ist doch ein Junge!" shouted a Gestapo man. It's just a young boy! Very scary moments followed while Ernest negotiated with the Gestapo man. Eventually, the policeman calmed down and Ernest was allowed to return. The train entered into Oldenzaal, Holland.

Ernest's passport photo (1926)

In Oldenzaal, the refugees were greeted by a special committee with great pomp and ceremony. For their reception, tables were laid out with food and speeches of welcome made. Then women and men were separated and placed with Dutch families. A 13 year old boy, son of a priest, was helping my mother with her cases. Malka was taken to a little Dutch house where she just collapsed in front of the family and couldn't stop crying all evening. The lady of the house was very kind to her. She listened and comforted her.

"Why don't you stay with us?" she said to Malka. "I would love to adopt you as my third daughter." They became very close during the few days that my parents stayed in Oldenzaal, waiting for their transport to England.

I still possess my father's passport. I can see that crucial stamp:

'Grenzübergang Bentheim / ausgereist 31.3.1939' –
Bentheim Border / travelling out on 31.3.1939.

That ridiculously young looking photo of 16 years old
Ernest could have stopped my parents' journey and everything
would have been different. Or rather – there would have been
nothing, that whole branch of the family would have been cut
down. In his passport I can also see a stamp – the permission to
land at Harwich on 2.4.1939 'on condition that the holder does not
remain in the UK longer than three months and does not enter any
employment paid or unpaid'.

My parents, together with Kurt and Fritz, arrived at London
Liverpool Street Station. Another committee was waiting there for
the refugees and they were taken across Blackfriars Bridge to a
restaurant. Again women and men were separated and nobody
knew where the others were. Ernest – for some unknown reason –
was taken back across the bridge. This caused more stress and
anxiety for Malka. Surrounded by hundreds of other dispossessed
women, she spent a restless night. Next morning, however, Ernest
found Malka and they have stayed together ever since.

Although clouded by constant worries about their families
back at home, their English years were happy ones. I don't know
what my parents' initial months were like, but by January 1940, my
father had already started work at the Anatomical Institute of
Oxford University with Prof J Z Young. His research concerned the
effects of long-term denervation on human muscle and the ability
of peripheral nerves to regenerate. The topic was relevant to the
treatment of war injuries: when nerves are severed, muscles
waste away. His project was also the starting point for his later
work at the Institute of Physiology in Prague. My father's
enthusiasm for the studies of neuromuscular interactions started in

Oxford. He imbibed the atmosphere of frank and fervent discussions surrounded by excellent co-workers such as Peter Medawer, Ludwig Guttmann and Andrew Huxley. Ernest completed his PhD thesis in 1943 and remained working in Oxford until May 1945. My mother worked whenever she could as a helper to a General Practitioner in Oxford.

Malka and Ernest in New Marston, Oxford, 1940

My parents made many friends, both Czech and English and the friendships of the Czechoslovak refugees often lasted for life. I remember many of these friends; their children eventually became my friends and our friendships also lasted for life. There were also some relatives who lived in London. One was cousin Kurt, the one whom my parents met on the train when leaving Prague. Kurt eventually married Blanche, a Jewish girl who lost most of her family in a blitz. The other relative was Ernest's maternal side cousin, Elisa. She came to England as an au pair girl in 1938 and in due course married Sunay, an Indian doctor. My parents were close to and often met with both these cousins. My sister was born in Oxford in Sep 1941; Elisa's son was born that same year. There are numerous photographs proudly showing off the offspring to the world.

Just after Victory in Europe (VE) Day, 8th May 1945, Ernest told his cousin Kurt he was going back to Czechoslovakia.

"Why?" asked Kurt. "Here - the sky is your limit; everything is going so well for you! And there – the situation is unstable – the Soviets are breathing down our backs! Are you crazy?"

Kurt couldn't understand his idealistic cousin, who wanted to go back to his homeland to build a new, fair society. But Ernest insisted and returned - initially to work as a doctor with the survivors in the Theresienstadt concentration camp. He was there from May to July 1945, during the time of the Typhus epidemic. The epidemic spread through the camp due to the arrival of thousands of prisoners coming from the concentration camps in the east.

Meanwhile my mother, who was pregnant at the time, moved to London with my sister. They lived in Hornsey Lane, in a flat of her friend who had returned to Prague already. These must have been difficult months, a small child to look after, pregnancy, uncertainty. Communication with her husband was very limited. One day a lady appeared at her doorstep bringing a doll from Ernest for the baby-to-be (for me!). Her name was Marianne. She had worked as a nurse in Theresienstadt and met Ernest there. Marianne decided to come back to Britain. She kept in touch with our family all her life.

Marianne's 75th birthday in 1994

I was born at the Hammersmith Hospital in November 1945. At that time, my father was fighting for his life. His illness was due to an infection caused not by the Typhus of Theresienstadt, but by a dissection at the General Hospital in Prague - Vinohrady. He was so ill that he couldn't even send a congratulatory telegram from Prague to London. His brother Pavel did that for him.

Because of his German Medical Diploma, his not quite perfect Czech and his Sudeten background, Ernest couldn't find work easily. After six years of occupation, Czechs distrusted anybody even vaguely related to anything German. Thus the post of pathologist in a dissection room was the only job he could get. His infection developed into sepsis and fever. His life was saved by penicillin, then a new drug that was extremely hard to get hold of; a Hungarian friend managed to get him some.

My uncle Pavel, Ernest's brother, was a great help at that time. Pavel survived the war by escaping to the East. He joined the Czechoslovak Army Unit in Soviet Union and met his future wife, Jusia, in Czernowitz (Chernitvtsi), Western Ukraine. She was staying there with her relatives after having lost most of her family. She was only 16 years old and very beautiful; it was love at first sight. Jusia joined Pavel in the army as a telephonist and after the war, the couple returned to Prague together. Eventually, Pavel became a Major in General Svoboda's Army and a leader of the Army Artistic Ensemble. What was it like when the two brothers finally met? Try and imagine.

Jusia and Pavel, August 1945

It was my uncle Pavel who visited Malka in London after I was born; my father was still too ill. Pavel also helped my father to find an apartment in Prague. After he had recovered, in February 1946, my father finally returned to London.

"He brought only one suit with him" my mother told me "and right away I knew he wanted to go back to Prague."

Ernest was, in fact, very indecisive about what to do next: London or Prague? Prof. J.Z. Young, who was at the University College London at that time, offered him a job and a place to live. Mother, a great anglophile, was delighted with the offer and very reluctant to go back.

"We were so happy here" she reminded him.

"We were, but I feel I belong there. So much needs to be done to get things right again! There must be a way to do this!"

"It's going to be difficult, how will we manage? What about the children?"

"But I don't want to feel like a bloody foreigner for the rest of my life!"

My parents argued this way and that and finally Ernest said "Let's ask our daughter Sandra!"

He turned to my four year old sister "Shall we go to Prague? What do you think?"

"Yes, yes, let's go to Prague please!" she shouted - all excited.

On the 3rd of May 1946, the family returned. Kurt and Fritz came to the airport to say Good Bye. "You are meschuge, crazy!" were their parting words.

***

"Where did I bring the children to? My heart sank when I saw the airport full of human wrecks, ragged refugees, misplaced persons......"

The return to Prague was a shock for my mother. Full of foreboding, she followed my father to the apartment that Pavel

37

found for us. It was in the so called 'Little Berlin', in 'U Smaltovny' street. There was a welcome dinner waiting for the family, courtesy of two Jewish sisters living next door.

Later on, the two ladies took Malka to the nearby Veletržní Palác (The Trade Fair Palace).

"There across the street was the place where Jews were collected for deportations and marched off to the Praha Bubny Station" they explained. "For most of them it was their last walk through Prague."

That was all too much for Malka. She collapsed and cried and lost her breast milk because of all the stress.

"You got a ghastly diarrhea then," my mother told me forty years later. "You just wouldn't or couldn't get on with the formula milk."

Most of Malka's and Ernest's family members perished in the holocaust. Gradually, my parents found out the gruesome details of their fates and it took decades before at least some of these stories filtered down to us, the children. Those few remaining relatives became very precious to us – uncle Pavel and his family, the far away uncle Josef in Israel, and a few cousins of my parents.

Subdued conversations in English or German were the norm – at the time I thought that's what parents do. It was only the very beginning of trying to understand the incomprehensible. On the subject of holocaust there was mostly silence. Our Jewish identity was surrounded by mystery and unease. No Jewish holidays were celebrated at home although most of my parents' friends were Jewish and their interest in, warm feelings towards and affinity to all things Jewish were clear enough even to us, ignorant children.

Prague Bubny: ' Brána Nenávratna' was erected in 2015

Our family soon moved to Schnirchova Street, very near to the Praha Bubny Station, from where nearly 50 000 Jews, including my grandparents and uncles and aunties, were deported. It took 60 years before a poignant memorial to these people was raised there. It is called 'Brána Nenávratna' – 'The Gate of No Return' – showing rails directed to heaven and perhaps also a Jacob's ladder to heaven.

My parents wanted a new society, in which race and gender didn't matter and everyone had a fair chance. They were determined to get on with the work and make things better. That's why we were all back in Prague and, even though this utopia didn't work out, I consider myself incredibly lucky: growing up in Prague surrounded by history, beauty, poetry and magic was a huge bonus.

FAIRGROUND

May 1953

I shall always remember that day. We had just finished lunch and sat around our solid brown table in the large entrance hall that served as a dining room. Two matching sideboards and a grandfather clock surrounded the table, giving an impression of enduring safety and stability - except that there seemed to be an argument going on. Mum and Dad were talking very fast in English, impossible for us children to understand. Suddenly Mum banged the table.

"Come on children! Get ready! We are off to the fairground!" Her voice was unusually loud and resolute.

"You are just panicking" Dad said, "but have a nice time!" He withdrew into his study that was also my parents' bedroom. He drew the curtain that separated the study-bedroom from the living room and soon we could hear the clicking of his typewriter.

"What did he mean by 'panicking'?" I asked.

"He doesn't want to take off his rosy spectacles- that's all!" Mum muttered. And then – "Hurry up, get ready, Helena! Quick!" she shouted.

"I think he just wants some peace and quiet," my sister Sandra said. She knew these things, she was my older sister. I was only seven years old.

Sandra and I helped David with his socks and shoes. He was our little brother, not quite four years old and too impatient to get dressed on his own. Mum brushed our hair; a side parting on the left and a hairpin on the right to hold it back, no fringe, no fuss. Our hairstyles were similar, but Sandra's hair was always longer than mine – that wasn't fair! Just because she was four years older than me?

It was a warm day at the end of May, we didn't need any coats, just skirts and blouses and knee-high socks. We ran down the four flights of steps and hurried the length of Schnirchova Street, which was lined with 5-6 storey apartment blocks similar to our own. We turned left to Strojnická Street and before long reached the 'Julius Fučík's Park of Culture and Recreation' or 'Youlda Foulda' for short.

In front of the imposing 'Palace of Congresses', previously 'Palace of Industry', there was the fair. We had been there many times before to enjoy a fun ride or two, but this time was different.

"You can have as many rides as you like," Mum said. "We have plenty of time and plenty of money! You can go again and again." She laughed forcefully as she waved a pile of notes in her hand. "What do you want to try first? Merry-go-rounds? Swings or slides? Bumper cars or a helter skelter? Or perhaps the Russian wheel? Whatever you want, go for it!"

The Palace of Congresses in Youlda Foulda

I had never seen Mum in such a bizarre mood before, laughing hysterically, flaunting her money. Quickly, before she could change her mind, I decided to go on the merry-go-round and sit on the white horse. I encouraged David to come along and sit next to me on the black one. We climbed onto the horses while Sandra chose a silver carriage behind us. Up and down the horses went. We waved to Mum and shouted at each other.

When the ride finished, Mum, still holding the pile of money, was chatting to a lady in a beautiful blue polka dot dress. The lady's daughter was standing by, biting huge chunks off an enormous ball of pink sugar wool, her sticky fingers dangerously close to the polka dots. Moravian folk songs boomed from the amplifiers placed high on lamp posts, competing with the music from the carousels.

"You might as well throw it in the air!" shouted the lady so that Mum could hear her above the noise of the fair. The lady's matching blue handbag was half open and I noticed that it was full of banknotes. "Do you need some more?" the lady asked and offered Mum a stack of money from her bag. "My daughter is tired out, she has had enough." Indeed, the girl looked pale and her expression was that of boredom in spite of the delicious fluffy sugar wool in her hand.

"No thanks," Mum said. "I'm trying to get rid of it!" She turned to us. "How about some ice cream? What flavour do you want?"

"Chocolate! Vanilla! Strawberry!" We raced to the kiosk, gobbled up the ice cream and looked for the next attraction.

"Don't make yourself sick!" Mum shouted after us.

David's face was smothered with chocolate as he climbed into one of the bumper cars dragging me behind. Sandra and Mum watched us bumping along while they savoured their strawberry ice cream slowly, in a more gracious manner.

Why are we allowed all this? I was thrilled to bits, but also confused and worried about the way grownups behaved. There were groups of them everywhere, whispering, debating, gesticulating. I even saw one old lady crying. Still, the excitement prevailed over the worries. Sandra, David and I tried nearly all of the attractions at the fair and ate more ice cream and nougat than ever before. We stayed until the fairground closed for the night and went home with armloads of gingerbread hearts.

Too full and tired to have my dinner and too excited to sleep, I lay in my bed watching a beam of light coming through the frosted glass into our bedroom. I listened to the muffled sounds behind the closed door. Again, an agitated conversation went on between Mum and Dad, but radio news was on and I couldn't make out what were they talking about. Images of Flying Cages and Swing Carousels stirred in my mind. I was too scared to go on those two rides today, perhaps next time, when I got older, I would. Sandra and David were fast asleep already. The white horse with me on top floating up and down, up and down, came to my mind. David, on the black one, went the opposite way, down and up, down and up. We clasped hands midway. Scraps of my parents' conversations blended in with these images. I disliked those secret hushed exchanges. I imagined some unspeakable problems surrounding my family. Sometimes my parents whispered, sometimes they shouted, often in German or English, so we couldn't understand. Unnerved, I closed my eyes and pictured David's happy, chocolate-covered face as he manoeuvred his bumper car, shouting "Come on, come on!" Finally I fell asleep.

There was a lot to whisper about on that particular Saturday night at the end of May 1953, as I learned later. Mum and Dad would have argued about the so called 'Currency Reform' that was, after numerous denials by the communist government, finally announced on the radio that evening.

Mum would have said "I told you so!" and Dad something like "Perhaps it's for the best? I don't know any more."

Money lost value overnight; most people's savings disappeared. Soak the rich. Whatever was left of any private business collapsed. Everything became more expensive. Soak the poor too. In Pilsen and elsewhere there were workers' riots, soon suppressed by the police and the army, leaders brutally punished.

In my mind, however, this dubious step towards the building of a fair society was forever connected with the fantastic day at the fairground where, just as Karl Marx would have wished, each child was provided according to his needs.

PARADISE IN SUDETENLAND*

1950s

My kingdom could be entered by invitation only.

Twigs wedged into the ground and decorated with blueberries outlined its borders. Hannah and Maroushka had their own kingdoms too. We invited each other for tea and played hostess. The most popular game was 'How a Prince Charming courted a Princess'. In strict rotation, one of us became a prince, the other a princess and the one left over was a royal parent, whose job it was to make the prince's life as miserable as possible. When finally, after many obstacles, the time for the wedding arrived, there would be a feast of blueberries.

Wild blueberries were plentiful in the woods. We knew the good bushes by the reddish colour of their leaves' undersides; blueberries from those were the sweetest. Some berries were still green and hard but most of them were ripe and would burst in our mouths, colouring lips, teeth and tongues. And clothes too – but that didn't matter. Our uniforms for the wet summer days were grey, worn-out baggy tracksuits and black rubber wellington boots.

This holiday paradise in the Jizera Mountains was once part of a bustling village where Sudeten Germans lived and worked, many of them in mountain glassworks. After the war most of them were deported as an upshot of President Beneš's decrees*. In the early fifties, our parents bought some of the houses abandoned by the Germans to make them into our summer holiday homes.

Our parents were Jewish holocaust survivors. Since those few remaining knew each other well, the message about the abandoned houses got passed on in a sort of chain reaction. So it happened that the neighbourhood on that specific hill was soon nicknamed 'The Jewish Hill'. We, their children, were the products of the postwar baby boom. We didn't know much about the holocaust or the Sudeten Germans. We couldn't comprehend the link between our absent grandparents and the deported Germans, in whose houses we would now spend our summers.

Although the Jizera mountains are only some 60 miles away from Prague, in the fifties the journey there was a major adventure. It could take the whole day: trains, buses, trams and finally a walk up a steep forest path. On that hill, everybody knew each other. We could run freely from one cottage to the next, always welcome and often invited to have a taste of something or another: sugared blueberry dumplings swimming in melted butter or a freshly baked blueberry crumb cake, juicy as well as crunchy, or just a slice of rye bread covered with home-made cottage cheese.

Our cottage; the dry toilet at the back

Each house had its particular smell. Dry toilets and cellars were the most challenging parts. Looking down those deep toilet holes was scary – what if I fell right down? Or what if someone crawled up and pulled me into that muck below? The cellars were full of spiders. Sometimes I was sent down to fetch something from there, butter or milk – we didn't have a fridge yet. I carried a torch and trod carefully. I knew that both toilets and cellars could be closed from outside with a latch. It was great fun to lock someone in there - as long as it wasn't you. Usually boys did this to girls and girls to boys; the war of the sexes was on already. Milan, Michael and Vladimír were three particularly vicious boys. They were a big worry for us girls, Hannah, Maroushka and me. They spied on us and mocked our games meanly; sometimes even attacking us with nettles and chasing us out of our kingdoms.

Hannah and the boys

Many cottages deserted by Sudeten Germans didn't find new owners and lay in ruins. These became great places to rummage through. The excitement of such treasure hunts brought boys and girls together; gang fights were momentarily forgotten. No thoughts were spared for people who had to leave these houses behind. Heaps of beautiful glass buttons could be found all over the place, miniature glass slippers, glittering medallions and long coloured glass rods out of which buttons used to be made. All sorts of glass animals and vases and beads could be discovered. Together we plundered in blissful ignorance of Konrad Heinlein, the Munich Agreement and annexation.

Maroushka and Helena

On that hill, Maroushka was the only non-Jewish child and the only child with grandparents. Her granny was a big short lady who could hardly move, while her granddad was a tall and wiry man. He looked strict behind his round rimmed glasses but really was very kind. He wrote a play about fairies for us girls to perform. Hannah was a fairy of the meadows, Maroushka was Rusalka, a fairy of rivers and streams, and I was a forest fairy. The granddad painted the scenery sets and arranged them on a nearby flat rock. The granny made our costumes. It was a great success; even Milan, Michael and Vladimír were impressed and their teasing diminished.

On those rare sunny days, we would walk into the woods to watch the bright rays piercing the bristly pine branches. They made dappled patterns on the fine grass and the mossy boulders in the woods. We girls had a secret place there, close to a small stream. Underneath a large stone, positioned three steps left of a remarkable hefty rock, a small glass bottle lay hidden inside a plastic bag. It was wrapped in several layers of cloth and inside lay a piece of paper carrying a message: 'Helena, Hannah and Maroushka are friends forever'.

Somewhere here was the secret place

Each summer when the holidays started, after making sure we were not followed, we visited this spot. We inspected how far decay had set in over winter and, if necessary, revamped the message.

Neither Hannah nor Maroushka nor I can now recall how it happened that one year we invited Milan, Michael and Vladimír to witness our silent ceremony. The boys stared at the exposure of the decaying paper in silent admiration. After some grave negotiations – we'll never again do this, you'll never again do that - a new message was placed inside the bottle: 'Helena, Hannah, Maroushka, Milan, Michael and Vladimír are friends forever'.

And we were, our friendship has lasted till now, though none of us remembers any more how and why that hefty rock was remarkable.

The Sudetenland were areas along Czech borders, mainly inhabited by ethnic Germans. After the creation of Czechoslovakia in 1918, Konrad Henlein (1898-1945) became a leader of the fast growing Sudeten German Separatists Party. In September 1938, an agreement was negotiated in the absence of Czechoslovakia at a conference held in Munich. The Munich Agreement, permitting the Nazi German annexation of Czechoslovakia's Sudetenland, was signed by Germany, France, the United Kingdom, and Italy. Today, it is widely regarded as a failed act of appeasement toward Nazi Germany.

In response to Nazi occupation (1939-1945), Beneš Decrees laid the ground for forced deportation of approximately three million Germans from postwar Czechoslovakia.

ZDENA

1959

Maroushka's mother, Zdena, was a young widow still in love with her late husband. She was highly emotional and melodramatic, feminine and sexy, romantic and giggly, simply a great contrast to my Mum's no-nonsense attitude. Cropped trousers showed off Zdena's shapely legs, wavy dark hair tied back away from her face emphasized the dark questioning eyes. She and Maroushka spent their summers in a holiday cottage that was only five minutes away from ours. Maroushka and I were playmates.

Zdena and Maroushka and other kids

Zdena's little red rucksack was always at hand, packed and ready to go. She loved to be with us, the girls, inventing adventures for her daughter and her band of friends.

"Shall we have a picnic by the river?"

"Shall we go for a swim at the Lido?"

She invented poetic names for her favourite places such as 'Eagles' Nest', 'Black Tarns' or 'Rusalka's Rocks'. Marching us kids off to these destinations, she sang old songs from the first republic times: songs about tramps who steal chickens and roast them over an open fire, about cub wolves who are not afraid of anything, about nine canaries that can't be paired up. Or she would sing those sentimental ones about hideaway cottages where he is going to kiss her while a wild river roars in the lap of rugged mountains. For us girls who were brought up on propaganda songs about how to tether wind and clouds and how to order them when to blow and when to rain, or on songs about factory chimneys that ooze smoke towards heavens making the sun blink, but not to worry since everybody in the country will now have a better tomorrow, for us girls Zdena's songs came as a breeze of a mysterious promise, a possibility of adventure and romance, a message from another world.

"Girls," Zdena proclaimed, "You must look after yourselves. Your skin starts ageing after fourteen." Thus cleansing and moisturizing became almost a religious duty for me, particularly because my mother never mentioned such trivia. Zdena talked about massage oils and fragrances, about how to treat hair with egg yolk, yoghurt or dark beer and complexion with cucumber peels, all this in a secretive confidential tone as if conspiring a regime change.

Zdena adored both my parents and often sought advice from them, particularly on medical matters. She would come running down the steps towards our cottage.

"Imagine, Malka, I couldn't sleep all night, my back is killing me!"

My Mum may have just settled down to enjoy her well-deserved rest after having cooked lunch, cut the grass and tidied the front hall. If sunny, she would have been in the garden, stretched out on a blanket in her shorts and her bra, sometimes even without - for the entire world to see.

"Mum, please!!!"

"What's the matter, Helena? I haven't stolen anything from anyone!" She would dismiss my objections. As soon as Zdena appeared, whatever she was doing, Malka would jump up and talk to her, pat her on the shoulder, give reassurance.

"Take a hot bath, have a good rest, it'll get better."

Ernest and Malka in Janov

Another time Zdena might hold my father's hand, her eyes brimming with tears.

"Ernest, my dear, what a disaster! I've had a migraine for three days!"

He would listen sympathetically to her problems, half concerned and half amused, definitely charmed, looking at her through his solid, thick rimmed glasses. There was a kind of innocent special relationship between him and Zdena. He loved the role of a protector, the role that was difficult for him to perform at the side of his practical and unwavering wife.

"Hmm, I think you should see a specialist. Shall I arrange an appointment with Dr Such and Such, a neurologist? He's very good."

"Oh, Ernest, thank you, you are an angel!"

My mother was not one for walking; she had a weak heart and too many things to do around the cottage. Thus, on those rare occasions when he could take time off, my father would join Zdena's expeditions into the hills. Sometimes, he and Zdena liked to pretend they were the long suffering parents of all those wild teenage girls, four or five of us, with an odd brother or two thrown in. They got lots of sympathy from other hikers as they invented tales of woe about the problems with their unmanageable kids: truancy, laziness, obstinacy, impulsiveness. It was such a hard life, they complained. I wasn't sure did my father mean it? Was I really so bad-tempered and stubborn? Or - on the other hand - maybe I was boring him because I was insufficiently naughty? I was confused; better to monkey around with the girls than to worry about such things.

Later on, Zdena acquired a lover, a Mr Zelenka. He was much older than her, had glassy blue eyes and somewhat devious manners. Zdena invited us for tea to meet him. Duly, he tried – feigning an accident with his tea cup - to put his hand on both Maroushka's and my knees under the table. We just wriggled and giggled while Zdena served the biscuits but as soon as he left, all of us fell about laughing.

"Did you see the way he looked?"

"He spilled his tea all over himself!"

"He slobbered and pretended he was offering me biscuits when he did that!"

There was nothing sinister in it, no fear, no threat, just the hilariousness of the situation that we shared together.

"It's nothing serious," Zdena said about Mr Zelenka, "he's just a companion." Her eyes looked dreamily at us as she sighed. "Sometimes I need someone to make a bit of fuss on my behalf, to take me out to dinner or to a concert..... but obviously, he could never be my partner – could he?"

I loved the confidences with which Zdena entrusted me. It made me feel grown-up and equal and helpful. With time, hysterical giggling over Mr Zelenka changed into more focused discussions about men.
"Watch out, Helena!"

Thus it was with Zdena, rather than with Mum that I could discuss these matters. Perhaps emotions were just too dangerous for my mother, who after all had lost so many of her nearest and dearest, perhaps that's why she had to keep her feelings in check.

And so it was Zdena who knew how to ask.
"Well, Helena, what was it like? Did he kiss you yet?"
Zdena allowed my suppressed doubts and angsts to come out into the open from behind the 'Keep Smiling Gate'.

THE LITTLE VIXEN

1959

Dear Diary, imagine! It was my 14th birthday yesterday and father took me to an opera. I hope you don't mind – I have decided I'll write in here as if I am talking to someone. And that someone will be you, my dear diary. Well, it was my first time for the opera. But not only for the opera, also for suspenders. What a scream it was, me wearing a suspender belt! I could feel the knobs that held up silky stockings underneath my red woollen dress. The dress had an embroidered black velvet collar which made me look quite sophisticated and grown-up. Even father noticed it, I think. In addition to his usual silly jokes such as reciting "Helena goes to an opera, in her red dress et cetera", he looked at me and declared: "Not bad, let's go and show them!"

Prague National Theatre was as grand as I expected. At school, we covered its history loads of times. How in the mid-nineteenth century the nation collected money to build a Czech theatre: 'Národ sobě' - 'The Nation to Itself.' How it burned down only a few months after its opening and how the collections started all over again. Now I could see it in all its glory: lights glittered, angels fluttered, chandeliers glowed, muses descended from the ceiling and the walls. I saw people in elegant evening attire and worried whether my red dress would do. I asked my father "Do I look okay?" but he was intent on finding his friend Gustav.

"Ah, finally, there he is!" He was so relieved to spot him.

Oh no! I realised that Gustav had brought his son Joseph. My parents think Joseph is a paragon of virtue but I find him unbearable. He is just one year older than me, but believe you me, my dear diary, in his dark suit and a tie he looked like an old man.

He gave me a feeble smile and then continued to read his Programme. Gustav and Dad were deep into a conversation so I looked at the Programme too. The opera was 'The Cunning Little Vixen'. Adventures of a Fox called 'Sharp Ears' by Leoš Janáček. Some kind of kid stuff, I thought and resigned myself to boredom for the rest of the night.

We settled onto the red velvet seats, fathers in the middle, Joseph and I well apart. The lights went down. Reluctantly, I watched the sleeping Forester surrounded by dancing animals in the woods. However, as soon as the little Sharp Ears appeared, almost against my will, I was entranced.

"What is it?" the vixen shrieked when she first came across a frog. "Nice to eat?"

Dear Diary, I must tell you that when the little vixen got caught by the forester and lamented in her courtyard prison, "Oh, oh!" the music was crying with her. When she finally escaped, the music was soaring to the heavens and I felt her delight so keenly that I considered myself to be one with her. It could well have been me who brought havoc into Forester's quad, killing all the chickens and biting the silly, lazy dog. It could have been me escaping from there and kicking the badger out from his home. I was happy when later on the vixen met a handsome young male fox who courted her. The vixen sang "Am I really so beautiful?" and he admired her like mad. Dear Diary, it was lovely!

During the interval, I looked for any signs of admiration, but there were none! Dad bought me a chocolate ice cream and asked me how I liked it.

"Very tasty, thank you," I said. And I told him how I love the vixen!

"Oh good!" he said, but soon continued his intense discussion with Gustav. What did they talk about? I strained my ears and could hear the names of Khrushchev, Camp David and Eisenhower but I couldn't make any sense of it.

The Cunning Little Vixen

Meanwhile, Joseph decided to tell me all about his latest Internal Combustion Engine Model Kit. He waved his arms around and raved about moving pistons, camshaft and timing belt. Luckily he had finished his ice cream already. While explaining the firing of the sparking plugs, he went quite frantic but at that point I had had enough. I stared at him.

"Am I really so beautiful?" I said. "Did you like the fox singing it?"

"Yeah, it's a nice dress," he went scarlet. "Oh, the fox, you mean? Yeah, she's okay, yeah." He started to read his Programme again and I went back to my seat to have a good look around.

I ran my fingers over my thighs to feel the suspenders and turned my eyes towards the muses and the angels. Staring up at the ceiling, I got dizzy from all the lights and the gold in circular layers. On the painted curtain, scantily clad people were shown to be intensely debating something that I couldn't understand either.

There was a lady, perhaps an angel, flying in the air, her white robe fluttering. I waved to her before the curtain lifted.

Prague National Theatre

I was sad when after the interval the vixen died and the little fox cubs lost their mother. At least, before she died, she trained them to be vigilant. I wasn't sure why that frog appeared again at the end of the opera. Why did it jump at the forester, who was now quite old? I asked my father about it on our way home.

"It was a different frog" he said. "A grandson of that first frog, you see? Life goes on." Then once again he turned to Gustav to talk about silly Khrushchev.

In the tram Joseph sat next to me looking dejected. My dear diary, do you know that I felt sorry for him? A little guilty for embarrassing him, I tried to make amends.

"Joseph, have you got a chemistry set?" I asked him. "I've got one for my birthday."

It worked, his eyes lit up. "Have you? And what's in it?"

I told him about growing beautiful crystals from copper sulphate solution and making Bakelite from polyvinyl acetate adhesive and borax. He got really excited when I mentioned coloured smoke and sparklers and suggested he could come and help me to set it up. Well, what could I do? We made a nebulous arrangement for next week. I'll tell you all about it later. My dear diary, although Joseph dresses like an old man he is still very immature, don't you think?

LET'S DO IT
1964

In the last year of High School, boyfriends were the main topic of our conversation. All of my friends seemed to have one, all except me.

"May I ask you for a dance?"

These words, spoken under the glittering lights of sumptuous chandeliers were loaded with indefinable promise - so far unfulfilled. The Prague Municipal House was a place where we had taken our dancing lessons, it was a norm. After acquiring appropriate skills we could show off at various Leavers' Balls, the so called 'Maturita Balls'. We glided cheerfully and hopefully in the arms of numerous young men with flushed cheeks and sweaty hands.

"Do you come here often?"
"I am sweating like a pig, how about you?"
"And so - what do you study?"

Oh please! I wanted to speak about books, arts, theatre, poetry, or at least about mountain tracks and campfires! Encouraged by the sensuous paintings and adornments on the walls of that exuberant Art Nouveau building, I continued to whirl and swirl in eager anticipation. The Prague Municipal House resounded to the tunes of twist and charleston, foxtrot, tango, waltz or rumba, jive or cha cha cha or samba, even polka or mazurka, I loved them all. I danced enthusiastically and listened with admiration to the idols of the day: Yvetta Simonová with Milan Chladil, Eva Pilarová with Waldemar Matuška, Hana Hegerová,

Václav Neckař and so on; their songs permeated my brain indelibly.

"Would you like to come to the Semaphore Theatre with me?"

Just as my expectations were at the lowest ebb, Paul appeared! I had met him before. It was exactly a year ago and at the same place. We had danced and even talked about books together, but nothing happened, although my hopes were raised. We recognized each other immediately. He was tall and handsome, with an attractive ironical smile, witty and not over-pushy. What luck that he should come again to my Ball! I was a great fan of the Semaphore Theatre and knew how difficult it was to get the tickets.

"I would love to come" I said and that's how it all started.

Paul was already past twenty, a student of Building Engineering, while I, at eighteen, was just preparing for my final high school exams. I wasn't sure about what to do with myself afterwards; my parents – as could be expected - promoted medicine. However, I had read a book about Louis Pasteur entitled 'Fighting Invisible Enemies'. Ever since I had wanted to study natural sciences.

We discussed exams, families, ideal societies, books, poetry, films, theatre, and our plans. When spring came along we met more frequently. We wanted to be together but there was nowhere we could go to, restaurants were too expensive, theatres too. We just roamed the streets of Prague until late. We could ride trams or buses to explore remote corners of Prague suburbs. We could sit on the benches of the Petřín Park looking at the castle lording it behind cherry blossoms or we could just walk by the river watching the shimmering city lights reflected in its depths.

Poet Macha's memorial at Petřín

"Where have you been?" Mum asked.

"With Paul."

"Is it getting serious? You are much too young!"

I couldn't talk about Paul with Mum or Dad. Emotions were a taboo at home; everyone was too busy and too uncomfortable to talk about them. One was supposed to be all right; one got on with things and kept smiling. And I smiled a lot as I looked at the world through my rose-tinted glasses.

Inevitably, in due course my overblown ideas about love led to bewilderment.

"You are not listening to me."

"Sorry."

"No point saying sorry if you don't mean it."

"Don't be like that..."

"Like what?"

"What's the matter with you?"

This discontent was confusing; it didn't fit in with my notion of love. I read poems and novels about it and made copious notes in my diaries, but there was no one I could talk to.

"I'm sorry I snapped at you. I was upset."

"You can be very moody, quite irritating with your needling and sneering."

Whenever I had had any doubts about Paul, I blamed myself for being unable to love truly and selflessly.

In time our meetings extended to weekends and then weeks away. Discovering the countryside and wandering around the mountains was our shared interest. Rucksacks with a few essentials, good boots and off we went. Paul was in his element, an enthusiastic man of action, always finding the right way over hills, through woods, lighting fires, building a tent for the night or finding a perfect barn full of fragrant hay for a sleepover. I loved our wanderings.

In Prague, however, I was getting frustrated with Paul's lethargy. Perhaps I was just too energetic for him. I initiated most of our outings to plays and films and lectures, dragging him along. I questioned whether his devotion to me was more to do with inertia than with appreciating me for who I was. Again, I condemned myself for wavering. I continued meeting Paul at assorted corners of Prague, brushed my doubts aside and looked at the bright side.

I met his family, he met mine. We had known each other for over a year now but still had nowhere to go to be together. Our romantic walks through the city were beginning to consume too much of our precious time, which we both needed to study. Paul was preparing for his state exams and I was in my first year reading chemistry. Even if we had the money to do so, there was no possibility to simply hire a room somewhere and live together. There was no such option in the 1960s Prague. We could only hope for an apartment if we got married.

"Well? Why don't we just get married?" Paul was by then nearly finished with his studies and was looking around for a suitable job. "I have a friend at the Council and he could help us to get a flat."

"But you'll have to spend a year in the Army."

"I know, but the longer we are married the better chance we'll have of getting the flat."

"So really, nothing much will change after the wedding – I'll stay at home and you'll be away – God knows where - somewhere in the Army."

"Time will work for us though."

"Well, let's do it! Mum and Dad can't stop me now that I am over eighteen."

"You can't be serious, Helena! You're much too young!"

"But we want to, Paul and I want to get married."

"Don't be silly, you are still a student! Where will you live?"

I explained our wicked plan to apply for a flat and told them how after his one year in the Army, Paul will get a job and will be earning.

"You're much too young!" Dad said.

"Helena, don't you want to think it over?" Suddenly Mum sounded anxious, but there was no way back. The excitement of it all overwhelmed us.

The date was agreed and the preparations started.

WORK EXPERIENCE IN AMERICA

1966

Many strings had to be pulled for me to have work experience in America. In the mid 1960s, a student from socialist Czechoslovakia journeying to capitalist America was something unheard of. However, this was the time of relative liberalisation and things unheard of became possible.

My parents befriended a family of an American scientist who knew the Czech Minister of Culture who, in turn, knew someone at the Foreign Office. The American scientist arranged an invitation for me to work over the summer in the laboratory of his colleague. This was a beginning of a long process.

To start with I had to prove my positive attitude towards socialist causes. This meant that I had to fill in countless questionnaires. Then I was challenged by a handsome activist in the blue shirt of the Czechoslovak Socialist Youth to join the Communist Party. I thanked him profoundly for the honour of this invitation. In a well rehearsed double-speak mode, I excused myself by saying that I still felt too immature to make such an important decision. We'd better wait until I became a responsible adult. The young man played my game and let me be.

As a next step, an invitation came from the Ministry of Foreign Affairs to attend an interview. I was led through the long corridors of power to meet a motherly lady, whose task it was to warn me of the dangers of the decadent capitalist society. I'll be surrounded by an extravaganza of consumer goods that mask dreadful inequalities and poverty. New York is the city of rampant crime. Rapists and thugs are wandering the streets and I'll have to be very careful. I nodded seriously but in my head I laughed, thinking it's just a load of propaganda. We never believed anything official, whether in papers or on the radio, and particularly from people at the ministry. Passages from 19th century rural novels came to mind. I imagined that in Austro-Hungarian times a young village girl must have been sent to serve in sinful Vienna with the very same words.

Then I had to deal with the U.S. embassy. Their questionnaires explored whether I ever was a member of the Communist Party. No, I assured the Americans. I was simply a student of Natural Sciences given this unique opportunity, from which I'll benefit hugely. Enriched by my American work experience, I'll come back to my family and finish my studies.

I got my American Visa and a three months' work permit. I got the obligatory permission to travel from the Czechoslovak government. My passport was ready. I couldn't believe my luck: off to America, the land of plenty, the land of rock and roll!

I was introduced to Martha, a young girl who also planned to travel to the United States. She had an invitation from some family members in Utah. Martha and I decided to travel together by train and boat; in those days it was cheaper then flying. On our way to the port of Cherbourg we stayed in Paris, where Martha had an aunt. This aunt was a grand and extravagant lady who liked to dine her way through innumerable courses, which she cooked effortlessly. She taught us how to eat oysters - still alive. After dinner, in the middle of the night, she took us out to wander through Paris.

Paris! It was my first Western City. As a teenager, I had devoured novels of Balzac, Hugo, Flaubert, Rolland. Paris figured highly in all of them. Now I feasted my eyes, overwhelmed by actually being there. Both familiar and exotic, Bois de Boulogne, Champs-Elysées, Madeleine, Sacré-Coeur, the names alone were pure poetry to me. I visited the Louvre – of course – and bought some postcards of Michelangelo's sculptures.

After a few days in Paris, Martha's aunt took us to Cherbourg where we boarded the liner Queen Mary II. Yes, the sumptuous Queen Mary II. Hard to believe it now, but it's a fact. The voyage took 6 days. We spent them lounging, swimming, reading and staring endlessly onto the vast, ever-changing ocean. We had never seen an ocean before.

Mealtimes were the highlights. One morning the sea was rough and nobody except us turned out for breakfast. People were just too ill to eat. Soon one other couple appeared. What a surprise, they were also Czechs, American Czechs. He used to be a diplomat and she was a charismatic, mischievous lady, very 1930s, and very supportive of us, two greenhorns. These two old-worldly, first republic people, knew the first Czechoslovak president, T. G. Masaryk, and talked about him with a great affection. The bourgeois president – that's all that we, the children of the revolution, knew about him.

The drama of the approaching Manhattan skyline exceeded all our expectations. Everybody was running around the deck with a camera. The city looked like a spiky monster from the distance, then like a cluster of stalagmites, then like a cavern getting closer and closer to us.

Queen Mary II

There was no problem with my passport, but a custom official spotted my postcard of Michelangelo's sculpture. It was called 'The Night' and showed a naked woman fast asleep.

"Why do you carry this with you?" he stopped me.

"It's art," I explained patiently.

He observed me with an increased interest and showed the picture to his colleagues: wink, wink, ha ha ha. Then he noticed a large red apple that I had snatched from the bar.

"No food allowed, sorry".

"Can I eat it now?"

I couldn't bear to leave the juicy apple behind. He agreed and I ate it there and then, choking under his probing stare. After I had gobbled it up, I was finally allowed to enter the capitalist den. Martha and I said Goodbyes. She married a Mormon in the end and stayed in Utah.

Montefiore Hospital, Bronx, my place of work, was a huge red brick building. I found the doctor who was to be my boss on the 2nd floor. He took me to the lab and patiently explained the aim of the project: to analyse steroids excreted by humans.

"Yes, in shit," he confirmed. "Don't worry, you won't have to collect it. You'll only work with the final phases of the extractions."

Dutifully performing all the tasks given to me, I did my best to understand both the science and the language. My evenings were spent exploring New York, wandering across its grid at random, clutching my English dictionary, straining my neck to gaze at skyscrapers.

Initially, I stayed with my parents' friends in the affluent New York suburb of Scarsdale. Every morning I walked to the station to catch my train. I was often stopped and asked whether I was all right, perhaps I needed a lift? It seemed I was the only person there who walked.

"No, thank you, I'm fine," I proudly explained. "Just going to catch my train to the Grand Central."

The Grand Central! I loved the sound of it.

Later on I lived more centrally. A cousin of my Scarsdale hostess was away on holidays and I could stay in her flat on 89th Street. It was just round the corner from the Guggenheim Museum and close to Central Park too, a good place to go for a morning jog I thought.

"Helena, are you crazy?" Inge, a kindly German researcher at the hospital took it upon herself to protect me. "You can't run in Central Park, there are dangerous people there! And you can't walk at night on your own in New York!"

Inge was so exasperated she told the whole lab about it. She even phoned my hosts in Scarsdale and they were horrified. I was told off. My Scarsdale friends used words not too dissimilar from those of the matron at the Czechoslovak Foreign Office.

To be sure, after some unpleasant encounters on the streets of New York my cockiness disappeared. I had to be careful - there were rough no-go areas. Although supermarket shelves were overflowing with goods, I saw real poverty, for which I wasn't prepared. As people loaded their shopping trolleys, I thought of my mum chasing for food from one shop to another, waiting in long queues and often carrying heavy bags up to the fourth floor because the lift wasn't working.

I realised that coming from behind the Iron Curtain, I must have seemed something like a Martian to people around me. The questions they asked! Are there humans there? Two legs? Two arms? Two eyes and one nose? Most of them thought I must be desperately miserable back at home and overawed by the freedom and the riches of the United States.

In fact, I thought my life in Prague was exciting, but very few Americans could understand why. How could I explain that the human face of socialism beckoned and that the Prague Spring and its idealism were in the air? Endless discussions about the merits of the socialist versus the capitalist system were exhilarating. We hoped for a change, for a new way.

"Do you all wear uniforms?"

"Yes, and shackles round our ankles."

"Do you have electricity?"

"No, wolves roam the streets of Prague and howl piteously."

So my reaction to New York was mixed. After the magical, sleepy, melancholy streets of Prague, I thought New York grey and aggressive. Its buzz and vigour were impressive but scary. The quantity of goods seemed excessive, wasteful and disorientating. Why is there so much stuff everywhere, I thought, while there are thugs, lunatics and vagrants on the streets? People work too much, I thought. Many people I met told me they were too busy to take holidays, women got only two weeks or even less for their maternity leave!

However foolish this may seem now with hindsight, supermarkets and department stores were not quite as exhilarating for me as our Prague debates on power sharing and democracy. When I returned home, they called me a naïve leftie.

BLOW BY BLOW

1968

Every citizen of what was then Czechoslovakia, who was then old enough to remember, will give you a blow by blow account of what he or she was doing on August 21st 1968, the day when the Soviets invaded the country. I can't leave my account of that day out, so here goes:

On August 21st, at four o'clock in the morning, Paul and I were out in the middle of a Russian forest, half way between Moscow and St Petersburg, mushroom picking. We were staying by the lake Udomlya at a cottage, a dacha, with Sasha, his wife Tatiana and a few of their friends. All these Russians were medics and all were eager to get into the woods as soon as possible. In Russia, mushroom picking is a sacred sport, a passion, a religion. We had to get up very early to beat others. No strangers were allowed to see our finds; they had to be well covered with grass and fern.

I met Sasha at the Prague Biochemistry Institute when I was a student working on my final year project and he was a visiting scientist. Both of us were fascinated by the events of the 'Prague Spring' and had countless discussions about them and about life in general. We became good friends and Sasha invited Paul and me to come to Russia in the summer and spend the holidays with him and his wife.

We were in the middle of nowhere; just the woods at daybreak, the lake and the morning chill. The dawn was just beginning. Mist rolled lazily over the dark water surface as the bird chorus gradually intensified. Soon shrieks of discovery resonated throughout the woods.

"What a beauty!"

"I got you my darling! Don't resist, come to me!"

"There are loads of them over there!"

There were cèpes, chanterelles and plenty of 'Cossacks', the red-hats that grow under birch trees. *All mushrooms are edible, some only once* – so they say. But we knew them well and the Russians knew them even better. Our baskets were full by sunrise. We settled down by the lake to have our well-earned picnic breakfast. Bread, cheese, pickles and thermos with hot tea were spread out on a white cloth. Grisha switched on his pocket transistor radio. Since we were far away from civilization, it was safe to tune into the frowned upon Radio Free Europe. And that's how we learned that troops from five Warsaw Pact countries had invaded Czechoslovakia.

Picnic in Russia

'.....*Soviet Press Agency Tass has announced that Czechoslovak government officials requested urgent assistance from the Soviet Union to defend the socialist gains of the working classes.....*'

74

'.....Four leading reformers in Czechoslovak leadership
including Mr. Dubček were arrested by Soviet airborne troops.....'
'.....Tanks are rolling into the streets of Prague...'

During the 'Prague Spring', we had been too busy
attending various meetings and enthusiastically discussing the
best and the fairest way to run the country. We didn't worry all that
much about the massive Soviet military exercises on our borders.
Of course we had known that our way wasn't popular with Mr
Brezhnev, but he had nothing to fear! Didn't our leaders reassure
him and explain that we are going to stick with the socialist way?
How naïve we were!

When we first arrived in Moscow, we were surprised. Why
did people tut-tut at us whenever they heard we were from
Prague?
"You are having problems there, troubles, not good!"
We wondered what they meant.
"There are no troubles!" we told them. "All is fine!"
Even then we didn't grasp the power of Russian
propaganda and didn't worry about the raised Russian eyebrows;
we were unable or unwilling to read the clues.

"Tanks are rolling over the streets of Prague!" I sobbed.
"No thank you, I can't eat anything"
"It's not so bad!" Grisha tried to comfort us. "We often
have tanks in our streets. Cheer up!"
Why couldn't Grisha and the others understand? As
further news established that the invasion really did happen, Paul
and I began to worry about what to do next. We discussed
emigration: we'll return to Prague and then...... England was the
obvious choice. That's where I was born and where I had some

relatives. The thought of going back to conformity, pretence and deception under the old regime was unbearable.

As we walked back to the cottage with our baskets of mushrooms, we told Sasha about our plans.

"I could never ever leave Russia" he said. "Whatever happens, I need her. I'd feel motherless. But I understand ….I am so sorry."

He seemed to be the only one in the group who could show any empathy but then, he had spent the last six months in Prague.

"Please don't talk about your plans in front of my wife" he whispered suddenly.

"What do you mean?" I asked horrified. "Tatiana wouldn't...."

"You never know…" Sasha said. "Better not to..."

Back in Moscow we saw newspapers full of photographs of weeping Czech women embracing Russian soldiers with gratitude. Where did those photos come from? 1945, most likely.

We arrived back in Prague, just four days after the invasion. There was a spirit of resistance in the air. I felt that it was wrong to leave now – like a rat leaving a sinking ship. We walked the streets and watched the Russian tanks manoeuvred by bewildered teenagers from Ukraine, Bulgaria or Kazakhstan. Feeling of rage surged through me; I could have murdered.

"Ugly cars!" I explained to Pepi, my two years old nephew.

"Ugly cars!" Pepi repeated dutifully pointing at them.

I volunteered at our district council to do whatever was necessary. They sent me to clear the anti-Soviet graffiti from the walls of a department store known as 'Brouk a Babka'. That wasn't very inspiring, but I was still reluctant to leave everything behind.

"I'd feel like a swine and a traitor," I said to Paul.

"Don't be ridiculous!" he said. "At least you won't be a harebrained swine! What future is there for us here, in an occupied country?"

I already had permission to travel to Germany to visit a friend in Heidelberg so my passport was ready. In Paul's passport there was still a valid permit for the journey to the Soviet Union (SSSR in Czech), and we simply faked it into the one for the German Federal Republic (NSR in Czech). Our parents didn't try to stop us. On the contrary, they thought we should act quickly. We bought two train tickets to Heidelberg.

"We may follow you soon – we are thinking about it" Mum said.

Back in our attic room in Prague – Nusle, our so-called apartment that we were so lucky to obtain after we had got married, we packed a small suitcase each. We then stuffed all possibly incriminating documents from various Prague Spring meetings into a bucket and burned them. Clouds of smoke were pouring out from our little skylight window, strategies for the socialism with a human face were up in the air.

On August 31st we stood at the station saying Goodbyes. Dry mouths, cramps in our stomachs, forced smiles - as if performing puppets were set into motion by some invisible force. Mum had pushed packed sandwiches and apples into my hand.

"When will I see you again? Who knows.....Good luck! Stay in touch."

"Give our love to Elisa and Sunay! And to Blanche and Kurt!" Dad hugged us. "And don't forget to write to us!"

We had a warm welcome in London from my relatives Elisa and Sunay.

Elisa was my father's cousin, Sunay was her Indian husband. Uncle Sunay phoned my parents in Prague to tell them we were all right, very generous of him considering how expensive international calls were then. However after one week of our stay in Hampstead, he thought that – in our situation - we had ideas above our station.

"You must get a job, any job!"

But we had hoped that we could do what we were trained for. We needed time to sort ourselves out. Every day we read adverts and dashed around London, Paul visiting architects' offices and I exploring universities. Uncle Sunay disapproved.

"The main thing is to start working, whatever it is! You can't afford to be choosy."

Sunay was not used to resistance. He ruled his household with an iron fist of an Indian patriarch. Elisa was afraid of him and avoided confrontation. She kept quiet, mousing around the house unobtrusively. We were their guests; we were in no position to argue. The atmosphere there became very oppressive and we decided to leave.

I wrote a letter to Uncle Sunay. In my clumsy English I tried to explain that we had found new accommodation. ... *'Thank you very much. We don't want to trouble you'*.... I didn't want to offend him. He was kind to us, enjoyed drinking sherry with us, pouring it out into cute Bohemian crystal glasses. He had taken us out to my first ever Indian restaurant. It was an adventure and a revelation. Fish in an edible silver foil! Ladies' fingers in a spicy tomato sauce, Peshwari naan with almond filling. Food could be as riveting and exotic as distant travels.

At a Help Centre in London, we were advised to contact the Hayward family from Wimbledon. The Haywards liked Czechs and offered to host a couple of newly arrived post-invasion refugees. They remembered with great enthusiasm a wonderful Czech au pair girl who had stayed with them a couple of years earlier. She had been bubbly, lively and warm, simply adorable. But we couldn't offer the bright and happy scenario that the Hayward family might have envisaged. We two were ignorant, confused and uneasy with them and with each other. The stress of the new situation put pressure on our relationship. The Haywards were kind and friendly, but I felt, or imagined, that they were disappointed with us – we could never match their lovely au pair girl. We were anxious to find our own place.

By the end of September, Paul found a job as a draughtsman in an architects' office at Bedford Square and I obtained a grant to start my postgraduate studies at King's College London. Thus the extra time we had gained with the Haywards in Wimbledon turned out to be incredibly helpful. We found a bedsitter in Highbury, Baalbec Road. Our landlady was a motherly Italian woman. She was amused by my culinary ignorance; with her benevolent help I managed to roast a chicken – a Thank You Dinner for the Haywards after we had invited them to inspect our new status.

As for Auntie Elisa and Uncle Sunay, we didn't dare to invite them to our skimpy bedsitter. We visited them in October with a bunch of flowers and a bottle of Amontillado and stayed on good terms with them.

What if my parents had stayed in England after the war? What sort of person would I have become? What if Paul and I had stayed in Prague after 1968? What would we be like and what sort of young men would our sons, Matthew and Oliver, have become? What if my parents had emigrated in 1968 for a second time?

ERNEST NORMALISED

1968 - 1977

"I can't do it!" Ernest asked Malka to get out of the train.

They had just arrived at Cheb, the westernmost station of Czechoslovakia and were on their way from Prague to London. In the morning they had said heart-breaking Goodbyes to their friends and to their daughter Sandra and her family. They had decided to leave because Ernest knew that sooner or later he would be in trouble. He had signed 'Two thousand words'- a manifesto published in June 1968, which appealed to 'workers, farmers, officials, artists and everybody'* to seize a great opportunity, to take 'our common aim into our hands,'* to shape socialism .... with a human face. After the Soviet invasion, rumours were flying about that all signatories would be arrested and thus many of them had gone into hiding. Ernest's prospects for carrying on with his research in Prague were bleak. Since he had several offers from his colleagues in England and furthermore, since David and I had gone there already, Malka and Ernest decided to go.

"I can't do it all over again!" Ernest said.

Tears were streaming down his face as he stood on a drab platform at the railway station in Cheb, gazing at the train departing for the borders. Malka watched her weeping husband and had neither strength nor will to argue. This was to be their second emigration; some thirty years ago they were fleeing to England to escape Hitler. During the journey to Cheb, Malka watched Ernest gazing at the beloved gentle hills of his country passing by. She understood how difficult it was for him to leave the network of friends and colleagues. He had built a team of enthusiastic and devoted workers over the years and Malka knew his loyalty was being tested to its limits.

"Let's check the time-table for Prague trains," she accepted the situation with a sinking heart. Ernest was still clutching his suitcase as if he might still change his mind and start running after the train.

"It's all right, we'll go on living. It can't be so bad," Malka said.

But it was bad. Just a few months after the Cheb drama, people at all workplaces were asked to formally express their approval of the entry of Soviet tanks into their country - or - lose their jobs. The 'Normalisation Process' had started. Apathy spread through the country like a poisonous fungus and those who resisted the regime ended up as street- sweepers and window-cleaners.

Ernest tried to face it scientifically. He kept a diary where he wrote down his thoughts and observations.

"The similar pattern of behaviour of dictatorships through all times is remarkable. It suggests that we are dealing with some biological mechanisms, perhaps fixed genetically? Who would have thought that the most awesome and depressing material for such 'behaviour studies' would be presented by the so called socialist society? What a fantastic training for opportunism... .....how long can this go on?"**

It went on for twenty years. Malka kept her head down; she carried on with her work and her undying support of Ernest. For him "normalisation" started with a summons to the Presidium of the Czechoslovak Academy of Sciences, where he was asked to renounce his signature of the 'Two thousand words'. He was told "those who maintain their wrong standpoints cannot be directors or members of the scientific community."**

Ernest tried to argue with them. "This wholesale revoking, now a routine activity in this country, is totally demoralising!"** A number of bizarre disciplinary committee meetings followed. He tried to keep his calm by reminding himself that "the people in charge are actually liars and they know it."** He tried to behave "as a cold observer who may have been asked to write a chronicle."**

The attacks and the insinuations that he could not be trusted continued. A series of meetings resulted in disciplinary warnings, appeals and finally, in April 1970, in the expulsion from the Communist Party. This was done almost apologetically by a cheerful gentleman who confided to Ernest. "It would have helped us if you had retracted. We do understand that intellectual pride is involved. We would have given you the disciplinary warning only, but – sorry comrade - you just made things too difficult for us."**

Ernest noted a feeling of satisfaction. "The shock changed to a relief that one is no longer responsible for this devaluation of a party, which once had such a tremendous appeal to human dignity and hopes."**

Shortly afterwards, Ernest celebrated his 60th birthday at the family holiday cottage in Janov, in his beloved Jizera Mountains. It was the place to which he could escape and get away from the constant worries at the Institute. There he relaxed and indulged his hobby, painting. His affection for these mountains still glows from his pictures. The 60th birthday was a memorable occasion; friends and colleagues hired a bus covered with streamers proclaiming 'We love Ernest!' It made him feel that his efforts were not in vain. "The most important department is the department of human relations"** he noted down on that day.

Facing endless obstacles, Ernest kept working. He continued his research and wrote scientific papers although his contracts were now only short term: three months, six months, perhaps one year. Numerous days were spent compiling applications to prolong the contracts. He was not allowed to go to congresses, teach or accept any invitations or scholarship rewards. He kept his spirits up and never stopped being himself; the joke-cracking, witty, charming, self deprecating, forgetful professor. But the stress was taking its toll. In November 1976 he wrote: "The vague fatigue I feel so often is caused by this chronic uncertainty. Is it worth it? But that's just the price I have to pay for being able to continue working in my country."**

Ernest in the Golden Lane, Prague 1977

"Esteemed comrade director," half a year later Ernest was applying to the General Director of the Czechoslovak Bank for the necessary 'Promise' of Western Currency. Without the latter and the eventual exchange of the applicant's Czechoslovak crowns for the promised Western currency, it was impossible to travel. Thus, thousands of Czechoslovak citizens had to write such begging letters.

"I was informed by the Currency Promise Committee of Prague 7 that their Promise-designated Currency Stock had already been exhausted. Therefore I would like to turn to you with my application: I am a 67 years old scientific worker.......until now I have never asked for a Currency Promise.... I have not been abroad since 1969. My wife is a working pensioner....I wish to visit my daughter in London and meet my two grandsons, Matthew and Oliver, 2 and 4 years old, that I have not met so far....I would like to do so while my health still allows me....I ask you respectfully for a positive response to my application..."***

Surprisingly, both Ernest and Malka obtained their Currency Promises as well as their Permissions to Travel. In the summer of 1977 they set out for England again, this time with valid documents and suitcases packed with straw dolls, blueprint fabric, Bohemian crystal and wooden puppets.

***

"You haven't changed at all!"

Paul and I welcomed my parents with the obligatory courtesies, but they knew we didn't mean it. During the nine years that we had not seen them, they had aged considerably. It didn't matter - the excitement of the meeting was overwhelming. My brother David had just arrived from West Berlin and was already waiting for us at our house in Croydon. I served a festive dinner of roast beef and Yorkshire pudding to make sure everyone knew this was England, but only the children could eat. The adults were much too emotional.

"I feel I can breathe again!" Mum inhaled the Croydon air with pleasure.

"I see what you mean," Dad said. "Somehow the English air feels lighter. Still, Janov is Janov."

"Hope you all are well" Dad wrote from Croydon to my sister Sandra in Prague, "and that you'll stay at the cottage in Janov as long as possible. Here, everything is over-civilised; no real forests here!" ***

Yet, in the morning he always asked for corn flakes, bacon and egg, and toast with marmalade. He was basking happily in the sunshine at Trafalgar Square on the steps of the National Gallery and enjoyed a long leisurely walk across Hampstead Heath with his cousin Kurt.

Soon, a stream of visitors appeared in Croydon; the house was full of laughter and reminiscences. Invitations came from all over the country; one of them was to Grantchester near Cambridge to visit an old scientific colleague and his family. It was while driving back from there to Croydon, after a very English lunch in an idyllic summery cottage garden that Dad died suddenly of a heart attack. It was unexpected and traumatic, so hard to come to terms with and at the same time to deal with all the formalities.

Poor Mum travelled back to Prague with his ashes.

***

Gradually, things changed. After paying a sort of ransom fee to the Czechoslovak government, it became possible to 'legalise' one's stay abroad. Since 1981, my family travelled from London to Prague every year to visit our Czech relatives.

Mum moved to a smaller flat and continued to work as a paediatrician until her late seventies. She died two years before the 'Velvet Revolution' and never knew that in Prague one can breathe freely again.

* *Citations of the Two thousand words Manifesto*
** *Citations from Ernest's diaries and/or letters*
*** *Citations from Ernest's letters*
(my translations)

A FAMILY REUNION

1986

All together for a whole week! Mum, my sister and my brother, and the children - all together at our mountain cottage. Jizera mountains were my childhood paradise. It'll be good to get away from London. Even my nearly teenage sons, Matthew and Oliver, who normally play it cool, were excited. Mum was thrilled to bits in anticipation of seeing the children and the grandchildren all together. As soon as we had reached the cottage, she pulled out tins of home-made cakes and got on with spoiling the boys.

"Matthew, you'll love my chocolate pastries. For you, Oliver, your favourite poppy seed strudel." Mum, the unshakable Anglophile, relished the English conversation.

My sister Sandra drove from Prague with her children, Luisa, 12, and Pepi, a young man of 20. They arrived shortly after us in the early afternoon. Sandra was still dazed from the exertion of the drive.

"Jesus Maria, what a journey! I'm shattered" she complained. "Sorry, we can only stay for the weekend. Richard wouldn't like it if we stayed any longer."

"Can you stay until Sunday afternoon at least?" Mum was disappointed.

"Yes, we'll leave in the afternoon but not too late. How will I ever manage the journey home?"

"You got here all right," Mum said, "you'll be all right getting back."

"Forecast isn't too good for Sunday."

Sandra began emptying her bags: more cakes, walnuts from her garden, a leg of salami from her local butcher and finally a couple of jars of her own delicious jam.

"These are for you, sister, red current jam, I know you like it." She collapsed onto the sofa. "Heavy rain tomorrow, they say, just what I need!"

"Do you want to rest for a bit?" Luisa looked at her mother anxiously.

"No, I'll be fine, you two go and say hello to Matthew and Oliver. Let them practice their Czech on you."

At last my brother David and his wife Michiko arrived from Berlin with their little daughter Izumi. David's head was completely shaved; it glistened in the sun like a precious instrument.

"Finally! Here we all are!" Mum had a shock seeing her son's shaved skull, but put a brave face on it. After the usual welcoming rituals, she busied herself with tea cups and it didn't take very long before she pulled her rubber gloves on.

"Oh my, these windows need cleaning!" She set to work. "They haven't been done for ages."

We exchanged glances. Mum has always been good at keeping her chin up. No time for doubts or worries. She cleaned the windows for the rest of the afternoon, now and then examining their gleam with a smile of satisfaction.

"But Mum, this was meant to be our holiday!"

There was nothing for it but to help.

Meanwhile, baby Izumi charmed everyone around. She squealed with pleasure when Matthew, Oliver, Luisa and even Pepi played peek-a-boo with her.

"Look how affectionate they are with her!' My sister didn't miss the opportunity to tease me. "Wouldn't they just love to have a little baby sister?"

"No chance."

"You never know..." Sandra persevered.

"Look, it's not going to happen. I can assure you." I cut her short and handed her a squeegee.

The windows that didn't sparkle enough for our Mum looked out from the kitchen in three directions. On the left, one could see large stone steps descending the slope towards the entrance so that any approaching visitors could be spotted and welcomed straight away. Front windows looked into a small fenced off area with a couple of rose bushes, a bench and a picnic table. Behind the fenced-off area was the rest of the garden; overgrown grass, some fruit trees, even more neglected now than I remembered them, and a row of red current bushes. The grounds spread towards a stream that was surrounded by lush ferns. On the right, the windows were looking down towards the village of Janov and, in the bluish distance, the town of Jablonec. At night one could watch its glittering lights down in the valley.

After our exertion, we sat around the large kitchen table and contemplated the stone steps, the garden and the distant hills through spotless windowpanes. Thin green and white glass rods of a lamp shade above the table tinkled gently in the breeze. A few kitchen towels drying above the stove moved to and fro, keeping pace with the tinkle. We could have been enjoying each other's company and taking pleasure in the woods, meadows and bubbling streams outside. English, German, Czech and Japanese endearments could have floated in the air. Children could have played happily together while plates of blueberry dumplings with quark, sugar and melted butter were being laid out on the table. Many cups of tea, perhaps some wine. Happy, balmy summer days. But the idyll was not to be.

"How they have all grown up!" Mum said after the grandchildren had gone to bed. We settled around the table with our teacups, ready for a cosy chat.

"Matthew is almost a young man now, a born leader!"

"Oliver looks up to him, doesn't he?"

"They were so nice with Izumi!"

"Pity Luisa and Pepi can't stay any longer – they would have enjoyed being with their cousins."

The conversation continued to revolve around the children. David sat there quiet and uneasy until he got up awkwardly and excused himself.

"I feel rather tired - bed time for me, I think. Good night everyone."

After he had left Michiko stood up.

"Sorry to bring bad news, but David has decided to leave us," she announced all of a sudden.

We sat there dumbstruck.

"What happened?" Mum shook her head. "You can't be serious, Michiko!"

"I don't really know what happened," Michiko said wearily. She muttered something into her tea cup and began to cry. She couldn't stop.

"We are all very tired now," Mum said. "This must be some misunderstanding, surely! We'll talk tomorrow." She helped Michiko to her room.

"Helena, you must talk to him," Mum said when she came back. "Please do! I know you are close to him, you understand him!" she implored.

"Did you know about this?" Sandra inquired.

"I suspected there was some trouble brewing when I saw them in Berlin last winter."

"What trouble?"

"He is into Buddhism," I said reluctantly.

"So what?" Mum said cheerfully. "We can all live with that. Buddhism is very interesting."

"I mean he wants to become a monk."

"A monk?"

"A Buddhist monk?" Sandra and Mum cried out together.

"Yes."

"But he's got a child and a wife! You must talk to him tomorrow, Helena!"

"What do you want me to say? How can I change his mind?"

"He listens to you!" They both insisted.

"I can't talk him into anything. Who knows what's good for him?"

Mum knew.

"He should work for his degree and get a good career."

Mum's face brightened as she made up the list of joys so obviously available to anyone if only they got on with it.

"Interesting, rewarding work, family, home, daily routine...."

She was convinced he would see the light in the end and everything would be all right again.

Next morning, I observed Michiko as she fed Izumi. David assisted her as well as he could, but Michiko's voice was resentful and terse. She bossed him around.

"I want some tea!"

"Glass of water for Izumi!"

"Cut the apple!"

Quietly, David brought this and that, looking down, avoiding her eyes, as if he'd rather be on a different planet. I felt sorry for both of them. I could see that David was just as inept at home chores as our late father was. Perhaps, just like our Dad, he wanted to run away to an ivory tower somewhere.

Our father used to sit behind his massive writing desk, a God-like figure not to be disturbed. His work was his family. It was our practical Mum who, without much appreciation, kept the family together. However our witty and charismatic Dad reaped our admiration. His conspiratorial winks amused us more than Mum's woeful requests.

"Where do you think you are?" she always reprimanded.

"This is not a hotel! I can't do everything on my own," she implored.

"Come on children, let's get the dishes done - or else - we'll be in trouble." Father's meaningful sighs. "You know what she's like...."

He was lucky that Mum forgave him and never stopped caring. But then, she was lucky too, never a boring moment. He was absolutely charming and supported the family as well as his academic passions. She missed him terribly.

Since the children were around, we didn't return to the topic of David's leaving until later in the day, Michiko took me aside.

"Helena, talk to him, please. How can he behave like this? If not for me anymore, I know he really cares for Izumi."

"Michi!" I embraced her. "Do you remember when I visited you in Berlin two years ago? It's hard to believe things have changed so fast!"

At that time, David still had a huge head of unruly curly hair and wore colourful cotton shirts. He was tipsy with happiness, cracked jokes and spoke in rhymes. Michiko looked exotic and ageless with her long smooth black hair and elfin figure.

"I thought you were so good for each other..."

"Yes," Michiko sighed, "at that time I absolutely admired him, but now? What has happened to his charm? It doesn't work on me anymore."

"Why not? Has he changed?"

"I expected more!" There was anger and despair in her voice. "I am the breadwinner now, that's hard enough. True, he makes a tolerable house-husband while I am at work, but I expected more."

"Surely he will find a good job eventually, won't he?"

"He doesn't want to!" Michiko cried. "He says he has lost any sense of his life. He can't go on, he says."

"Perhaps he'll find it and come back?" I said tentatively.

"He's going to leave us and I don't know what to do. I feel so angry and let down. How can I face my folks in Japan? Shouldn't he take care of his family?" Michiko sank onto the chair and wept. "Is he crazy? A monk? And what's going to happen to us? How will I cope? Has he no sense of responsibility? Can't you talk to him?"

"I'll try, I'll see what I can do" I promised.

On Sunday morning Sandra was already packing her bags. She examined the sky for any sign of calamities that might befall them on their way to Prague.

"Jesus Maria! It looks quite black over there. Pepi, Luisa, we'd better leave early before the storm comes."

"It'll blow away, don't worry! Give the cousins a little more time together."

We all went mushroom-picking into the woods. I was happy listening to the Czech conversation that Matthew and Oliver held with Luisa and Pepi.

"Houby! Houby! Mushrooms!" Matthew and Oliver shouted. "We found some ceps!" They were keen to identify the edible ones and to learn their names.

"Ceps are the best!" Sandra said. "I'll cut them for you and dry them so that you can take the jar back to London." For a moment she forgot to worry about her driving. The family united over the mushrooms, discussing their names and habitat. Even Michiko and David joined in enthusiastically.

"We'll see each other back in Prague," Sandra said. "I hope all will go well here." She looked at David as she pushed Pepi and Luisa out of the door.

A few days later, after a restless night, both Izumi and Michiko fell asleep soon after breakfast. David sat with a book in the front garden. Perhaps now would be the good time. Matthew and Oliver were playing by the stream, Mum was reading the papers in the kitchen.

"David, can you spare a moment? "

"Sure, my dear sister, come and sit down."

He always liked to put on this over-courteous manner with me. He smiled and made space on the bench. His shaved head

95

was getting sunburnt and the skin on his skull was peeling. He wore black tracksuit bottoms and a plain white T-shirt. Next time it'll be orange robes, I thought. I knew that he was unlikely to share confidences with me anymore, but I still asked the question.

"David, do you know what you're doing?"

"Yes, Helena, I'm flying to Colombo in a month's time. All decided and fixed. Don't even try...."

"But what about Michiko and Izumi? And Mum?"

"I'll help as much as I can. But at first I'll be out of reach for some time - I'll be in a forest monastery."

"And if something happens?"

He gave me a piece of paper with the address of his guru in Colombo.

"Does your teacher know that you are married? And that you have a child?"

"Look, it is very difficult for me. You know that. But that's what I must do."

He smiled, tapped my hand briefly - a token of our previous closeness - and changed the subject.

"And what about you, Helena? How is it going?"

"Not so good."

I looked at him and wondered: is there any point in telling him?

"Paul and I are splitting up," I tried. "I've filed the divorce petition already. Mum doesn't know yet."

"Poor Mum" he said, but was too preoccupied with his own plans to enter into any further discussion.

Poor Mum. I needed to talk so badly - I had to tell her. I waited until the afternoon, when my brother and Michiko left with Izumi and the boys for a walk to the nearby hill called Královka. Mum was hanging out the curtains on the washing line.

"Can we talk?" I handed her a cup of tea and we sat down.

"Divorce? Are you crazy?"

Mother was convinced it was just one of my momentary upsets.

"You are just hypersensitive. Problems can be overcome."

She gave me examples of several long - suffering wives, including herself, who sailed through. She told me about Dad's occasional misdemeanours. How from time to time he used to come home all tearful to confess and how she forgave him and life went on.

"And look at Sandra! You know things are not easy with Richard, but they keep trying and are still together!"

"But Mum," I protested, "It's not just the misdemeanours. Our attitudes to life are completely opposed. Paul won't make any decisions now without consulting a Dream Dictionary! He believes all is pre-determined and spends most of his time interpreting signs."

"You must be tolerant!"

"I know - live and let live – that's all very nice, but he's pushing his crazy ideas onto me. How can I live with that?"

"Don't be silly. You know that family is everything. Love, loyalty, support, a safe harbour, companionship, forgiveness."

Mum's face lit up again as she envisaged these marital delights. I embraced her and we didn't talk about it anymore.

I walked fast and soon caught up with the rest of the family. David was in his funny, jokey mood. Izumi giggled away, entertained by her father and her cousins. We stopped for a drink and then continued on the ridge road, eastwards from Královka towards the Hrabětice village, admiring the stunning views. The Ještěd Mountain with its pointed tower was behind us, dark outline of the Krkonoše Mountains ahead, the town of Jablonec down below and the familiar landmarks of the Jizera Mountains to the north on our left.

"Those hills over there have such poetic Czech names." I pointed out the northern hills to Michiko. "Beautiful Mary, Dove Hill, Birds' Mounds, Snowy Towers."

"They used to have German names as well." David reminded us. "This was Sudetenland after all. So we could say we are walking from Königshöhe to Grafendorf and are looking down to Gablonz an der Neiße."

"How interesting!" Michiko was surprised. "I didn't know this used to be German. There seems to be no trace of it anymore."

"Oh yes there is!" David said. "You can still get quite a lot of Germanic ambience round here." He wrapped his arm around her shoulder in a conciliatory manner. "But things change – life is change, isn't it?"

Ještěd

The silhouette of Ještěd - Jeschken could now be seen black against the red western sky. It was time to go back; Mum was expecting us for dinner. Izumi was fast asleep in her pushchair as we walked home in silence.

THE NIGHT WITH THE COWBOYS

1987

The 'Great Western Rent-a-Car and Stagecoach Company' in Fort Collins offered a small Plymouth Champ.

"Yes, I'll rent it," I said. Just what I needed for a few days trip around Colorado. Overwhelmed by a mixture of anxiety and excitement, I paid the deposit. Anxiety - because my driving experience was minimal. Excitement - because after two months of hard work in a Fort Collins lab, the prospect of exploring the country was tempting.

I started to drive up the Poudre Valley on Friday noon, feeling like a pioneer facing wilderness. Keep to the right! The road wound up and up presenting dramatic views. Glorious autumn colours stood out against steely grey skies. Looks like rain....better stop for lunch before it starts.... maybe right here by the river. I unpacked my double-decker pastrami sandwich and contemplated my future. Perhaps the work that I had completed at Fort Collins, well nearly completed, would help me on my way. On my way to what? I had come to Colorado to develop a joint project with a colleague; its success would make a difference to my career, my badly needed independence. I'd be back in London in a couple of weeks. Back to my failing marriage and back to job-hunting.

The clouds darkened and I noticed the wintery bite in the air. I jumped back into the car feeling uneasy and wishing for company. As I manoeuvred the Plymouth Champ over Cameron Pass, it started to snow. I peered through swirling snowflakes straining my neck. Finally - thank God – there was Walden. Not a city as I expected, just a few houses in the middle of a prairie. Two motels to choose from.

"We are fully booked," a pleasant sixtyish lady informed me. "It's not normally like this" she apologised, "but this is high season, the Hunting Season, you see."

Indeed, both motels were full of hunters unloading their gear. Big guys running in and out with their guns, rifles, Gore-Tex and binoculars.

"Is there nothing else here?" I became despondent.

The kind lady patted my shoulder. "Why don't you drive over the Rabbit Ears Pass to Steamboat Springs?" she suggested. "They'll have vacancies there."

I panicked. "I couldn't possibly drive up into that snow! Not now, it's dark already!" I could feel tears were rolling down my cheeks. "Well, I just don't know what to do!"

"You can have a roll in my room," one of the hunters proposed, "you'll be quite safe with me and my son."

More panic. "That's very kind, thank you, but I think I'll have another look around the town."

The man's offer and my uncontrollable distress shook the proprietress into action. "Look, young lady," she said, "we have a spare bedroom at our house. Come and stay with us."

She introduced herself as Althea. A motherly type, her smiling face exuded care and concern. Salt and pepper hair was tied back neatly. She lived with her husband who was partially paralyzed by a stroke.

"We get up a lot during the night. You may not be very comfortable, but you'll be safe."

I cried some more - tears of relief. I embraced her.

"Thank you so much!"

That was the beginning of my night with the cowboys. We went to Althea's house where Vivien, a family friend, was waiting; she dispensed Bourbon on the Rocks immediately. Althea's husband Ken was upstairs but he soon banged the floor, asking for attention, he wanted to join us. Our idle talk wandered around ranches, cattle, size of bulls, trucks that drive thousands of miles to take the cattle to markets and competitions.

I listened wide-eyed, I really felt I was in Colorado now. A huge painting overlooked the living room: a bull, surrounded by a ring of snowy mountains.

"Where is that?" I pointed at it.

"I was born on this side of that bull." Ken laughed.

Conversation then steered towards Ken's Swedish and Vivien's Irish roots, while I mentioned my Czech connection. We talked about the children, husbands and ex-husbands, wives and ex-wives and finally about the troubles of Charles and Diana and the weather.

Vivien went home, Ken went to bed and I invited Althea out for dinner.

"Let's go to the River Rock Café," she suggested, "they have delicious scallops and chips and an excellent Coors beer."

Before long, Althea was driving with great confidence through the mushy snowy streets of Walden, heading to Main Street. She parked in front of the Cafe, a low, rustic style building full of logs, stones and antlers. While we were still browsing through the menu, I noticed Vivien entering with a whole crowd of people.

"We thought you'd be here!" Vivien laughed. "The word has gone round."

I was introduced to Vivien's husband and son and to Althea's nieces and nephews and cousins, as well as some hunters. All of them wore jeans and cowboy hats and were eager to meet the English lady with a funny accent who got stranded in Walden. Another group of hunters, hailing all the way from Mississippi, invited us to their large table. More drinks and cheek kissing, even hand kissing!

"You should stay for another day; otherwise you'll miss the taste of fresh elk steaks."

The Mississippi hunters smacked their lips noisily to illustrate how delicious these steaks are.

This time the natter was about hunting deer and elk and moose, about driving in a jeep and shooting, skinning, boning and quartering. They talked about the ways of freezing the meat and taking it back to Mississippi and about grilling and eating the steaks. Am I really part of this scene? I had to pinch myself. One of the hunter-cowboys grinned at me.

"Are you that lady who drove over Cameron Pass at 15 miles an hour?"

"It was at least twenty five!" I protested.

"I passed you very carefully."

"Thank you, that was kind." Everybody laughed and I giggled hysterically, feeling light and free.

Onwards to another saloon, the nearby Moose Creek Cafe with an enormous moose statue in front of it. Inside, two aging flower children who called their band "Prairie Moon" played country-folk. People on a large wooden dance floor swayed enthusiastically to their tunes. Althea's son Danny stood at the bar wearing a sweatshirt splattered with white paint.

Moose Creek Café in Walden

"You can't come in here like this!"

Althea pulled it off him quickly, exposing a T-shirt that declared 'COLORADO' in large blue capitals. Danny embraced his mother and announced to everyone he loved her.

Danny invited me to dance and then taught me how to drink tequila. "First you lick some salt, then drink a shot, then eat a lemon."

But I didn't finish the drink because a handsome cowboy, blond curls spilling out from under his wide brimmed hat, came along.

"Shall we dance?"

"My pleasure."

He grabbed me tight and stated "Here in Walden we snuggle."

"Well, then we must!" I laughed and we danced cheek to cheek.

"Are you a real cowboy?"

"Of course!"

104

"I always wanted to meet one"

"I have been one for forty five years and that's how old I am."

Just the right age for me; the thought flashed, but I curbed it quickly.

"That's hard to believe!" I exclaimed and continued to flirt for England.

I danced the night away, happy as a child, protected from the big bad wolf by my kind chaperone Althea. The two of us exchanged glances, reassuring each other we were fine and having a great time. Althea danced too, chatting all the time and proudly introducing me to all of Walden: look what I have found!

During a drunken discussion about different ways of life in different countries one cowboy got up and clinched his fists.

"I don't think much of the slushy English ways! Where would you be without us anyhow?" he proclaimed. A choleric type in heavy boots with large spurs.

"Didn't the English prove themselves enough?" I argued. "In the Second World War or in cricket for example?"

"Anyhow .... anyhow..." he babbled on. "Your streets are too narrow to drive a proper car through!"

I wondered what he would make of the crooked streets of Prague, but before I could say anything, his fists banged the table.

"There's nothing wrong with the American life-style!"

"No, no, I love it," I assured him.

Danny resolved the situation by asking me for another dance. He danced well, wept drunken tears and whispered into my ears how beautiful my green eyes were.

"Goodness! What happened to them? They used to be blue!"

We got back to Althea's house in the small hours. I looked into the mirror and my eyes were shining, happy and sparkling green. It had been so long since I looked like this.

"It can be done, you see?" I told myself and crawled into a clean crispy bed.

I woke up with a hangover which soon lifted together with the morning mist. Althea made pancakes with maple syrup followed by delicious elk sausages.

We exchanged addresses, knowing that the likelihood of another meeting was nil. I felt sad to leave kind-hearted Althea and Ken behind.

"Good to meet you ma'am, you bet!" Ken shook my hand firmly.

Althea and I hugged.

"Thank you. You have done so much for me."

At that point I didn't realise I couldn't thank her enough.

Being alone on the road again felt good. I steered the Plymouth Champ and couldn't help smiling; the car felt like an old trusted friend now. Off to the Rabbit Ears Pass that was still covered with snow and then down and down towards yellow flat grasslands with isolated ranches and huge, bison-sized cattle. Endless, unlimited space, anything was possible.

MIKE'S DREAMS AND HIS HERITAGE

1993

They met at a petrol station in Streatham three years ago.

"I haven't seen you here before, are you a new guy?" Paul was a friendly customer from the very beginning.

"I am only staying for six months or so, it's my gap year job," Mike explained.

"And then? What are you going to do?"

"Maths and Philosophy at Bristol University.....it seems...."

"You sound a bit hesitant."

"I guess that's because I am. Well thanks.... see you soon."

Paul used to come at lunch time when business was quieter. He showed interest in Mike's uncertainty about his future and with time their chats in the petrol station forecourt became longer and more interesting.

"I was always good at Maths," Mike told Paul. "I enjoy a challenge, but somehow - my heart isn't quite in it."

"Work experience and a bit of travel will do you good," Paul encouraged him.

"Yes, it'll give me time to think things over."

"What do your parents think?" Paul asked. His manners were gentle and quiet. He spoke slowly, weighed his words and appeared to have a special understanding for Mike's situation. Although he was much older than Mike, perhaps in his late forties, they enjoyed each other's company.

"My parents are divorced. I live with my Mum. My Dad moved to Australia to live with his new partner. He does phone me often, you know, but our conversations don't amount to much. *So...how are things? - All right. - Good. - And you? - I'm fine.*

*Are you sure you want to take a gap year? – Yeah - Working at a petrol station - is that a useful experience?.......*You can imagine, can't you? "

"Sure!" Paul laughed. ""And your Mum?"

"I can't really talk to her about things. She's so proud of my maths skills, she thinks I'm some kind of genius. She'd get upset, she wouldn't understand."

"Bit of a pickle, isn't it?" Paul was sympathetic. Mike liked the way he listened to him.

One day Paul invited Mike for a drink after work.

"So – you are not sure what to do with yourself – that's OK, Mike, that's quite normal. But you know ....there is a path for every single one of us." Paul's voice became passionate. "That path, the path that God has determined for us, is often revealed in our dreams."

"What do you mean?" Mike was surprised. "You believe that God has plans for all of us? How can we know what they are?"

"Yes, I believe that. You see, we generally do things without thinking, just because it's expected of us. And then, perhaps too late, we may realize that it's not what we really want. Do you have many dreams, Mike?"

"Well, I do have dreams, but I don't remember much of them."

"It helps to write them down, Mike. Because, you see, in our dreams we get strong messages about God's will - if only we took notice of them!"

"But how can we understand those messages?"

"It's practice, Mike, lots of practice. And reading and contemplating. I've spent many years trying to understand these signs. They are sent to all of us, Mike, but sadly most people don't pay any attention to them."

They began to meet more frequently. Paul described his life story to Mike. He had been married for over 20 years, but the relationship with his wife Helena was very unsatisfactory. He didn't enjoy his job either; he felt like he was in a rut. All that had changed once he had begun to notice his dreams. His life took a new turn. Now he felt he was close to God and his life had a new meaning. It seemed to Mike that Paul was the man of wisdom he had been looking for. There was a special, unworldly aura around him.

"Paul, I too have a feeling that somehow I am on a wrong path. I have started paying attention to my dreams .... I'm keeping a notebook by my bed now. I have begun to write them down."

"Good idea, we'll try to sort them out."

"Really? Can I come and see you then? I mean when my notebook fills up a bit? Can you help me to understand them?"

"I can try....." Paul's kind fatherly smile was reassuring. "But it's not just dreams, Mike. Be more aware of everything that goes on around you. Sometimes there are things happening, innocuous events, strange coincidences; these too may contain hidden messages. Perhaps we can work together to find the right path for you."

Soon Mike needed a second notebook. He started visiting Paul and his girlfriend, Vanessa, on Sunday afternoons. The couple lived in an apartment near Streatham Common. Their place was small and neat, with only the essential furniture, no clutter, no books, no television, not even a telephone. Vanessa was a slight, delicate woman, unassuming and quiet. She was very welcoming, there was always something delicious on the table when Mike arrived.

"I had a strange dream," Mike was reading from his notes. "I was sitting behind the driving wheel in a blue car. The car was moving, but my hands were in my lap, not on the wheel..."

"Well, who was driving your car, Mike?" Paul asked. "The hands denote power and competence, but in your dream, they don't seem to serve you. Blue is the colour of inner peace. You see? The potential is there but you seem to let someone else take over."

Paul's pale blue eyes stared at Mike with sympathy. The three of them carried on reading their notes, drinking tea, eating cakes and talking. Paul and Vanessa pointed out many omens that only confirmed Mike's own presentiments. Studying was not what he really wanted. He understood that he must stay close to God and learn to listen.

"Where have you been?" Mum was getting worried about Mike's Sunday afternoon absences.

"With friends."

"What friends? Do I know them?"

"Mum..... I don't think I want to study Maths and Philosophy."

"Oh, you have had second thoughts......so what would you like to study?"

"I don't want to study."

"Is there nothing you want to study?"

"No, I just don't want to study."

"Oh my God! So.... what do you want to do?"

"I want to be close to God."

"But how will you do that? ..... God's path? .... God's will? But what about your will? Aren't you responsible for your decisions?"

Soon after this conversation, Mike decided to move out. He had a job after all so he could be independent. He wrote to Bristol University to cancel his admission place. There was a small bedsitter going quite cheap near the Streatham petrol station. Mike didn't tell Mum where he'd gone; she may try to dissuade him and he didn't want any diversions. His faith was passionate and sincere and she just couldn't understand. Mum said she didn't care whether God existed or not; she'd carry on just the same. That worried him – will she end up in Hell? Hell began to loom large in his thoughts and that made him even more determined to find the right way.

Mum was upset. "So now you are going to be a petrol service sales assistant for ever. Is that what you want?"

"Don't worry, Mum, I'll be all right."

"Where can I phone you?"

"There isn't any phone where I live. I'll phone you."

"Can I phone the petrol station?"

"No, please don't, that would cause problems. They don't like private calls."

The bedsitter was cramped and damp, but exciting – Mike lived on his own now, doing his own thing. He worked hard at improvements, put some shelves up, changed the lights, got a nice bedside cabinet from a nearby junkshop. A little notebook was always with him, either at his bedside or in his pocket. Suddenly there was an abundance of dreams; he usually jotted them down at breakfast. Small everyday things had started to talk to him too: shop signs, street names or overheard remarks.

Meaningful coincidences

Mike pondered their meaning while at work. The job was boring and undemanding, he had plenty of time to deliberate. The highlight of his week was Sunday afternoon with Paul and Vanessa. They said they were very proud of him. He was now driving his own car. They encouraged him to get rid of the few books that he possessed and recommended he should concentrate just on the Bible and the Koran. It didn't matter which – both of them share the same vision - there is only one God. Mike might also enjoy reading some works of Carl Jung, Paul suggested, since they discuss events connected by meaning, not by a causal line.

"We can't understand the world only by the intellect! " Paul maintained.

"That's only a part of the truth, a very incomplete part." Vanessa agreed.

"That's why we need to pay attention to dreams and meaningful coincidences – they will lead us to our spiritual awakening," Paul explained. "It's hard work, it needs a lot of concentration.....but it's worth it."

112

Mike got into a routine: work, dreams, work, dreams. Outwardly, not much more was going on in his life during the following three years.

****

One spring morning, his boss called.

"Mike, you are wanted on the phone. Make it quick."

It was Gertrude, an old family friend.

"Herbert died," she said, "last Wednesday. Poor Herbert, he didn't quite make it to the new millennium. You know we were old friends, don't you? ....He died suddenly, but then he was 87."

Herbert was a distant relative; Mike wasn't quite sure how they were related. As a child he used to visit Herbert with his parents; even then Herbert seemed so old to him. He lived alone in a small dark bungalow cluttered with furniture and books. Books were everywhere and Herbert would often pick one or the other to show Mike pictures of massive mountains or incredibly long-limbed monkeys or other amazing natural wonders. Herbert's knowledge was daunting but Mike wasn't afraid of him. He always knew Uncle Herbert loved him; now he felt sad and guilty for not visiting him for so long.

"Oh, I'm so sorry," he said.

"Mike, can I come and see you on Sunday?" Gertrude asked.

"Well....yes... what's it about?" Taken aback by her request, he panicked. Gertrude must have talked to Mum. Of course, she must have got the phone number from her! Who knows what they had talked about? It must be some sort of a plot.

"You see," Gertrude continued, "before Herbert died, he gave me a few of his possessions. Sentimental value only, family things, you know."

"Aha..."

"Well, as you know, Herbert had no family left. He thought you might like to keep them. In any case, there isn't anybody else. So shall I come next Sunday afternoon? About two o'clock?"

"I could come to you," Mike said quickly. "It's a long journey for you to travel all the way from Crickelwood to Streatham."

"Oh, I don't mind travelling! I feel it'll be my last gift to my old friend."

There was no way out of this. Reluctantly, Mike gave her his address. He tried to change the day to Saturday so he wouldn't miss his session with Paul and Vanessa, but no, she couldn't. Too bad! But he couldn't have said no to the old lady. Not really.

Mike pottered around, clearing up before Gertrude's visit. There wasn't much that needed tidying up, just a few clothes and some crockery. After meeting Paul, he got rid of his accordion and his paints; such hobbies seemed too distracting now. How was he supposed to deal with Gertrude? He bought some buns, apples and oranges and milk. He wasn't used to entertaining and certainly not old ladies! It was some four years since he last seen her – his life was different then with many more people around. Mum's friends were coming and going constantly. There were sleepovers, long dinners and Mum busied herself then even more than usual. Perhaps that's why those frequent visits irritated him.

He had phoned Mum a week or two ago, before Gertrude's visit was arranged.

"Hello Mike, how nice to hear from you" was her usual friendly greeting. It didn't sound right though. No fun. They used to joke and laugh together, but now she always sounded so sombre ...... Nearly two o'clock, time to go to Streatham Station.

.

Gertrude was late. It was almost three o'clock by the time she finally arrived. Mike recognized her immediately – she still had that sharp, penetrating, no nonsense look toned down by her kind and friendly manner. She had aged though and seemed fragile and tiny.

"Sorry you had such a long wait, Mike." She embraced him. "There were some horrible delays."

"Hello Gertrude, sorry your journey was so difficult.... Are you all right?" As they began to walk slowly along the High Road, Mike noticed she looked very pale.

"I'll be OK as soon as I get some rest; I'm just beginning to feel my age."

Back at his flat, Gertrude sat down ashen-faced, muttering something quietly while Mike kept arranging the cushions around her. Nothing else mattered now – she must get better. On an impulse he sat down beside her and held her hand, suddenly feeling a surge of compassion. They stayed in silence for a while. Gradually colour came back to her cheeks.

"Can I have some tea, Mike?" She smiled. "Can you hand me my briefcase?"

She pulled out the parcel from Herbert and handed it to Mike.

He stared at the old photographs in his hand, images of unknown people in unfamiliar places. There was a majestic looking dame with a huge hat standing next to a spa fountain. An old man with a long white beard was reading a very large book. A group of young people in elegant tailored suits, each with a yellow star armband, smiled into the camera.

"Gertrude, what am I to do with this? Who are these people? It means nothing to me. In fact, I don't even know how Herbert was related to me."

"Can I have that lovely bun with my tea? Thanks, Mike... and now listen." Gertrude took a deep breath. "Herbert was a cousin of your mother's father, your grandfather's cousin. I knew both of them very well, we grew up together."

"Did you know my grandfather then?"

"Oh yes, I knew him very well. And – if you must know – Herbert and I were childhood sweethearts. But it all ended very abruptly, as you can imagine."

"What do you mean?" Mike wondered.

Gertrude took another deep breath and gave Mike one of her looks.

Two hours later, Mike knew that Herbert helped his grandparents to emigrate from Germany in 1938. He also learned a little about Gertrude's fate. They went through some of the photographs together. Most of them were carefully labelled and kept in appropriate envelopes. Gertrude explained who was who, what they were like when she knew them and how and where they ended up.

"So really – without Herbert, Mum wouldn't have been born!"

"No, and you neither, of course. It was Herbert who persuaded your grandparents that they must leave with him."

"It's all connected, isn't it?"

"Yes it is. He was a great help to your family."

"Why didn't I know this earlier?"

"Perhaps you haven't asked."

"Gertrude, you must be starving!" Mike's head was reeling; he needed food and fresh air. "I know a cheap and cheerful restaurant nearby, The Lucky Dragon, it's near the station. Let me treat you. Do you like Chinese?"

"That would be very nice, Mike, I love Chinese."

Mike put a clean shirt on and helped Gertrude into her jacket. They walked together through the Common to the restaurant.

"Ah, spring is in the air!" Gertrude inhaled deeply. "What a lovely park and so close to your place. All is lush and green. Look, forsythia is blooming already!"

At the restaurant, she suggested sharing the dishes.

"Would you mind vegetarian?" Mike asked.

"No problem. When did you become a vegetarian?"

"Well, I'm not, actually. It's just that I'm off meat during Lent."

"Oh, I see," Gertrude smiled at him. "Have you become religious then? Do you go to church?"

"Well….no, I don't go to church……..but yes, I've become religious."

"Which church do you belong to?"

"No….I don't go to church….I just believe in God and want to follow his will…" Mike began to feel uncomfortable. "Have you spoken to Mum about it?"

"Of course I have, I often do, we are friends, you know that, don't you? You can't be surprised if I tell you that Mum is worried about you."

Her smile lessened the impact. She must have realised that Mike would prefer to change the subject.

"Tell me what your work is like."

"Well, it's a simple job, not very exciting, but it gives me independence and time to think."

The tension eased a bit, but Gertrude hadn't finished yet.

"Mike, you are a very gifted young man, why would God provide you with all those talents? You could easily do something more fulfilling."

Mike's flushed cheeks and his exasperated stare stopped her saying more.

Luckily, spring rolls and the 'Buddha's Delight' vegetables had just arrived.

The food was delicious and the conversation shifted to safer ground. Mike related some funny incidents with the customers at the petrol station, while Gertrude told him about the book of memoirs she was writing.

"I'd like to read it," Mike said.

"Shall I send it to you?"

"Yes, please do."

Mike felt in control again, thrilled about being a host to this elegant old lady, a long-standing family friend. He insisted that they share a red bean cake to put a sweet finishing touch on their meal.

****

Mike did not sleep well that night. Half awake, half asleep, fragments of Gertrude's stories appeared in front of his eyes. How her father was arrested one day and never came back; she and her mother waited in vain. How she, when only fourteen, left her home to spend years in hiding, crossing borders, relying on other people's kindness and learning to avoid those who could betray her. He dreamt of soldiers, snow-covered mountains, grannies packing suitcases, lost children crying. He thought of his grandparents and of Uncle Herbert's thoughtfulness. He wondered whether the path along which so many perished was the God's chosen path. Was that God's will? And how about now? His mate at the pump was from Somalia. He had lost his parents, they were just poor farmers. Did they deserve to die? Was that God's will? Mike was confused. Was he beginning to doubt? He'd talk with Paul and Vanessa about it.

"We are not here to judge," Paul said on the following Sunday. He and Vanessa were delighted to see him again. There was a pot of tea and a comforting, freshly baked marble cake on the table. Mike told them about his strange dreams and visions after Gertrude had left.

"It's just....I wonder... were all these people, millions of them, on a wrong path? What about all the Buddhists and the Hindus...are they all wrong?"

"As it says in the Bible," Paul quoted: "*it is impossible to please God without faith.... He rewards those who seek him**. We are not here to judge," he repeated.

"Pray and God will guide you," Vanessa said. "*The one who doubts is like a wave of the sea that is driven and tossed by the wind***" she read from another passage. "The prayer will give you strength."

"Your dream about mountains probably means that you are facing an obstacle." Paul had consulted his Dream Dictionary. "And the snow in your dream may represent a fresh start or purification. Does it make sense for you?"

"Yes, it does actually," Mike felt exhilaration flooding his entire body. "What about those soldiers?" he wondered.

"Soldiers usually mean that one is preparing oneself to defend his beliefs and values," Vanessa recalled. "What do you think, Paul?"

"I think in Mike's circumstances that may well be the right interpretation."

There was a lot to talk about. Dreams about old women with suitcases and those about crying children were absolutely loaded with meaning. Mike got home very late, tired but elated. Perhaps his confusion will peter out.

Back into his old routine, his sleep pattern settled down and his dreams became more familiar. Mike dreamt he had fallen into a deep pit at the bottom of which lay a large dry oak branch. A black spider was crawling over his white shirt. A young woman in overalls was driving a train with great determination, deliberately not stopping at his station.

One day a parcel arrived at Mike's door. It was Gertrude's book and an invitation to her book launch. He browsed through the book briefly, looked at the photos and put it on the top shelf. He phoned Gertrude to say thank you and to apologise for his absence.

"I have enjoyed our meeting so much," he said to her, "but I feel quite confused now and not ready for socialising."

"No problem, Mike," Gertrude assured him, "Just phone me whenever you are ready. I'd love to see you again."

"I will," Mike promised, "as soon as I get sorted."

"Good luck, Mike!"

Hebrews 11:6
**James 1:6*

A SOIRÉE

1994

Izumi was disappointed. Her father, Venerable Dharmakara, won't hear her play at a concert tomorrow morning. It had been a whole year since she last saw him and he had reprimanded her then for not practising enough. She was keen to show him how much she had improved.

"He'll be here tomorrow night," Michiko said. "Oh, Izumi.... Listen. He says he's really very sorry, but he has to give a talk in the morning. Why don't you go and practice your piano? You can play for him tomorrow night. We'll have a little soirée, okay?"

"Okey dokey, Mum" Izumi sighed and automatically went through the notes of Beethoven's '*Für Elise*'.

Next morning, the concert hall was full of mummies and daddies. Michiko and her partner, Uncle Maxime, were sitting in the first row applauding enthusiastically.

"Brilliant!" Uncle Maxime shouted as Izumi came down from the stage in her black velvet dress. His cheeks flushed, eyes shining, he continued clapping. "Magnifique!"

"Thank you," she said, but didn't look at him.

"Well done!" Michiko said.

Later that afternoon, Helga, Dharmakara's disciple, phoned.

"Michiko, your little daughter was wonderful! ....Yes, I was there but I didn't want to disturb.......Just to say I'll be collecting Venerable Dharmakara at 5.30 tonight so we should get to you at about 7 pm. Is that OK?.......... You are having a soirée? ....Oh yes, thank you, I'd love to join you! Shall I bring anything?"

Michiko spent all of the afternoon cooking. She chopped vegetables and prepared the batter, ready for tempura. Proud Japanese, she wanted to show off her culinary skills. Uncle Maxime, having laid the table, was relaxing on the sofa with a glass of his favourite Bordeaux. Izumi, still in her velvet dress, was on her mobile, relating the events of the day to her friend.

"No, he wasn't…. He couldn't…..Yes, I'll see him tonight, and he'll be staying with us for a few days."

The bell rang at 7 pm precisely. Izumi jumped and opened the door. Dharmakara, draped in orange, entered followed by Helga who carried his suitcase. The cotton robes looked incongruous with his middle-European appearance. Dharmakara's shoulders were covered by a thick, warm purple cloak. A woolly hat, also purple, was pushed right down onto his eyebrows under which his blue eyes smiled benevolently. There were sandals on his feet, but he wore thick purple socks to shield himself against the harsh Berlin winter. The strap of a large orange bag bore down onto his right shoulder.

Dharmakara removed his hat to expose the shaved skull and bowed to Michiko with exaggerated dignity. His smile became slightly mischievous.

"Good evening", he said. Then he bowed to Izumi and Maxime and handed his cloak and bag to Helga.

"Good evening Reverend Dharmakara," Michiko greeted her estranged husband putting a somewhat farcical stress on 'Reverend'. "Hello Helga, come in!"

"Hi Dave! How's life? boomed Maxime. "Cheers! Salut!" he lifted his wine glass.

"Please, be quiet," Michiko whispered.

"Can't I greet my old friend David?" Maxime protested and proceeded towards Dharmakara, ready to kiss him. Michiko pushed a stack of side plates into his hands.

"Could you please finish laying out the table?"

Then she showed Helga where to put Dharmakara's things for the night.

Helga, now burdened with the bag, the cloak and the suitcase, followed Michiko to the spare bedroom. In spite of her load, she smiled – happy to be close and helpful to her adored guru. The suitcase was particularly heavy, filled with many weighty books by ancient Buddhist masters. She took some of them out and carefully placed them on the bedside table. Then she took out the contents of the orange bag: more Chinese books, Dharmakara's mobile and laptop and a carefully wrapped present for Izumi.

Sri Lankan dragon

Izumi observed her father and remained silent. Dharmakara turned towards her.

"Izumi, I've heard the concert was a great success. Well done! You've been very good with your piano practice. But of course, practice makes perfect. There is always room for improvement."

He reached for the parcel that Helga was just bringing into the room.

"I have a little present for you." He gave the box covered with a silky blue paper to his daughter and watched her.

"Thank you" Izumi said.

She opened the box to find inside a Sri Lankan puppet. It was a dragon whose mouth opened to reveal a set of fierce teeth. She ran her fingers over them to feel how sharp they were.

"Thank you, that's nice!" She smiled at him briefly and turned towards her mother.

"Can I help with anything, Mum?"

"Let's sit down, the dinner is ready," Michiko directed everyone to their seats. She made sure Maxime sat as far as possible from Dharmakara.

"I'll join you," Dharmakara said, "but Buddhist rules don't allow me to eat after lunch, so please excuse me. Little nibbles are OK though." He looked at Helga who quickly reached for her bag and pulled out some nuts, fruit and bits of cheese.

"Glass of Bordeaux, hey Dave?" Maxime asked, trying to get up from his chair with some difficulty. "Let's drink to the good old times in Paris!"

Michiko pushed him back.

"I'll make some tea in a minute. Help yourself everyone, plenty of tempura, some fish and rice and here, these are crispy noodles with sesame seeds and soy sauce."

Izumi loaded her plate with huge quantities of everything available.

"I love this kind of food," she said to her father.

"Self-control and restraint are very important in our lives," he said, but his words did not prevent Izumi from stuffing her face. She asked for seconds.

"One day you'll understand," Dharmakara instructed her with a smile.

"Listen to your father's wisdom," Michiko said to Izumi and looked at Dharmakara as she placed a plate of noodles in front of her daughter. Then she got up to put the kettle on.

The dinner was completed with coffee and Helga's cake. Helga, ever helpful, started clearing the dishes, but Michiko stopped her, tapped her glass and announced:

"Ladies and gentlemen, Reverend Dharmakara!" She bowed deeply in his direction. "We are now going to have a little after–dinner soirée. May I present Izumi, our musician of the day!"

Everybody clapped and Izumi climbed up onto the piano stool. 'Für Elise' soon resonated through the living room, inducing a state of entranced admiration in the audience. Michiko could barely stop her tears of joy. Dharmakara touched her hand.

"She is very gifted," he said.

Maxime, still cradling his Bordeaux, was immersed in an intoxicated reverie and beat the rhythm with his foot. Helga's face was streaming with tears quite unashamedly.

"Oops!" Michiko whispered to herself. "That was a wrong note!" But Izumi, increasing her mistakes, her sweet smile now transformed into a scowl, hammered piano chords to generate loud and angry cacophony. She paused and stared at Dharmakara. There was silence.

At last she began to play again the final gentle tunes of 'Für Elise'. She then climbed down, curtsied, grabbed the Sri Lankan dragon and ran out of the room into her bedroom. Clutching her puppet, she threw herself on the bed and cried.

HOPE OVER REASON

1995

It was yet another wet February day in London. Grey skies, constant drizzle and penetrating damp and cold. The empty nest feeling I had had ever since my sons had left home still persisted and pushed my own temperature well below zero. Robot-like, I performed my habitual morning chores when I saw an Interflora van crawling slowly along our wind-swept suburban street. It stopped right in front of my door. It must be for the neighbours, I thought, perhaps it's their fiftieth wedding anniversary?   But the man with a bouquet rang my bell.

I thought of Daniel immediately and my heart was racing. Is it from him? I could feel blood rushing into my cheeks and I must admit I was overcome by a feeling of happiness. It's for me! Beaming at the delivery man, I thanked him and rushed into the kitchen to place the beautiful multi-coloured bunch into a vase. Why was I so happy? When I met Daniel, I wasn't even sure whether I actually enjoyed his attention. All the same, I stood in the kitchen grinning at the flowers and thinking what to do next.

I decided to phone him. If I acted fast, he'll still be at home.

"Hello Daniel. Thank you so much for the flowers! That was sweet of you!"

"What flowers?"

"The flowers you've sent me. They arrived this morning and they are beautiful!"

"Helena? Sorry, but I didn't! I should have done, I wanted to, stupid.....now someone else is chasing you. Wasn't there any card attached?" Daniel asked the obvious. I froze.

"Oh God, I am so sorry! How embarrassing! I just assumed... I didn't even look for a card ... Sorry Daniel, so sorry to have disturbed you."

"No, no, not at all, Helena, I really wanted....." I hung up, rushed to the bouquet and rummaged for the missed card. Yes, there it was!

'To our dear auntie Helena from Blandine and Pierre. Thank you so much for looking after us.'

How thoughtful Jacqueline is, always so considerate. But I wasn't pleased. I paced up and down the living room shaking my head, talking to myself. How awful! What an idiot! What to do? Here I go again, impulsive, intense, confused. I didn't even like him that much ..... I just wish.....I continued muttering, occasionally switching to Czech to explain things to Otto, my tomcat.

"Rozumíš tomu Otíčku? Can you understand this, Otto? Úplný idiot! You have to put up with an idiot!"

I met Daniel two days ago at Jacqueline's place in Clapham. My friend Jacqueline was going through a divorce and Daniel, a lawyer and a cousin of hers, was helping her. I was there to keep her two children, Blandine and Pierre, entertained. The three of us grownups were all in our late forties; both Daniel and I had gone through our divorces already. After they had finished the paperwork and I had put the children to bed, Jacqueline fixed a quick dinner.

"Let's have some fun now!" she decided.

She hummed to herself as she cooked and by the time hors d'oeuvres were served she was singing bawdy French ditties at the top of her voice. I was glad to see my friend relaxing at last and didn't mind her lack of restraint.

"There you are! There is life after divorce, you'll see!" I encouraged her.

Jacqueline drank and recounted episodes from her future ex's life.

"He cried and said his heart was big enough for two, would you believe it?" She giggled hysterically.

"He said I should fight for him! As if I didn't have enough to do, looking after our two kids! Incroyable!" She rolled her eyes to heaven.

"He told the children he still loves mummy very much, but that mummy doesn't believe him...... Of course I didn't!" She raised her glass. "To me!" Jacqueline pointed at the elegant green dress she was wearing. "This is new, very expensive but I'm worth it!"

Over the main course, coq au vin, Daniel talked about his married life.

"My wife was never ready in time. We always missed planes, trains, dinners, concerts, you name it. She couldn't keep a job. It was some sort of OCD, obsessive compulsive disorder." He talked quietly, looking down at his plate. "She panicked over trivia; I could do nothing to calm her, I really tried, I've put up with it for nearly two decades, but in the end I couldn't go on."

"Why didn't you have any children?" Jacqueline asked.

"She didn't want to have children, she said she couldn't cope..... Oh well, so much effort invested and nothing to show for it. I think she actually manages much better on her own although I do still see her occasionally to help with this and that... Never mind, life begins at forty. Cheers!"

"Cheers!" Jacqueline replied. "Salut!" She pulled out a bottle of Muscat wine for the desert.

"It is strange," I sighed over my crème brûlée. "I too was married for over twenty years, but there is no affection left. If anything, I am just thankful I've got nothing to do with it anymore. I mean with that occult and all that."

Jacqueline knew the background but, as could be expected, Daniel gave me a quizzical glance. I had to explain my story a little more. Something I have often tried to do but never succeeded.

"Sorry, Daniel, I don't know how to describe the situation. My ex became very religious."

"Which church?"

"No, it wasn't like that, he didn't go to any church, no, he created his own system using the Bible, the Koran and Carl Jung."

"Very strange!"

"Yes, it was. He claimed he could interpret signs from God; with deep effort and concentration he could understand God's will."

"Was he like that when you first met?" Daniel seemed very interested.

"With hindsight, yes, he probably was." I finished my dessert pondering on the question. "It didn't register with me at first. Perhaps I thought it was poetic.....I do love fairytales and legends but I am a scientist. I like crispness and rationality. To me all that stuff about deciphering God's signs was just nonsense."

"Incroyable!" Jacqueline turned her heavy eyes to Daniel. "Such a bizarre scenario, don't you think?" And to me: "You did have hard times, didn't you, ma chérie?"

"I didn't really know with whom I was dealing.... A man waiting for signs? No will? No responsibility? He'd have liked me to help with elucidating his dreams, but I didn't believe in it and I didn't want to spend all my time on that. What could I do?"

"You've sailed through it quite admirably," Daniel said.

"Well, we parted amicably, correctly, politely. We didn't even need a lawyer!" I smiled at Daniel although I felt intimidated by his staring at me.

"You seem to be a very self-possessed person, calm and composed."

"Oh no – I'm not that! I just keep my turmoil well hidden."

Daniel offered me a lift home, emphasised how much he had enjoyed the evening and "We should get together one day," was all he said. All of a sudden he looked weary, bogged down with his work and his problems, receding hair, grey suit. I wasn't exactly encouraging, but we exchanged phone numbers.

That was only two days ago. So what did my reaction to the flowers mean? I got through the day with this question turning over in my head. The awkwardness of my stupid phone call haunted me as I travelled to work, did what was necessary there, and travelled back again on a packed commuter train. I slept very badly that night.

Next morning it was Saturday. The rain was even more relentless; rivulets streaming down along the curb threatened to wash us all away. To clear my head, I had decided to go for a walk, never mind the rain. I was just pulling on my wellies when the same Interflora van appeared. The same man came to my door - this time with a bouquet of twelve red roses.

"You are very popular!" he laughed.

"Oh no!" I just stared at him.

"What's the matter?" he asked and offered his arm to support me. I must have looked as if about to faint.

"Are you all right? People usually welcome me with joy!"

"Yes, thank you", I whispered, closed the door and searched for the card immediately.

Otto astounded

'Dear Helena, are you free for dinner next Saturday? Sorry I was too slow. Yours in hope Daniel.'

How embarrassing! I didn't even like him and yet pressured him into sending these flowers. Red roses, for God's sake! He had no choice of course, what else could he have done? I paced up and down again, wondering how to respond. Can I accept his invitation? And he thought I was composed! He should see me now! Hair dishevelled, cheeks burning, I continued pacing around the house.

There is no harm in meeting him, I thought.... I know I tend to be over- critical. Let's look at the positive side of things. I started to count Daniel's plusses: He was kind. He must have had really hard times with his OCD wife and yet didn't make a melodrama of it. He was friendly, self-effacing, not boring. He didn't ask to marry me, he just asked me to dinner. And I have been on my own much too long. Then I remembered the terrible awkwardness of the circumstances. He's just trying to do the right thing. And he's not my type anyhow!

'Dear Daniel, Thank you for the beautiful roses' I tried to bring appropriate phrases to mind. 'I realize my recklessness has caused an embarrassment. It's me, not you, who should apologize! Let's just laugh it off and leave it at that. I had enjoyed the dinner at Jacqueline's, thank you for helping her, she needs it. Yours Helena'.

I stuck a first class stamp on the letter and ran out to post it before I could change my mind. Rather pleased with my decisiveness and tact, I hurried home to cuddle up with the cat, forgetting all about the walk in the rain.

"Otto, there is no point in getting into yet another muddle, is there?" Otto settled down on the sofa next to me and purred. I stroked his warm fluffy belly and envied him his blissfully serene life. "One day I'll be like you, Otto, making the best of my time from one day to the next."

Next Saturday, following several rather long phone conversations, Daniel and I met at the 'Outcome Uncertain' restaurant, just opposite the Post Office in Sparrow Street. We shared delicious seafood pasta and a bottle of Muscadet.

DROWN YOUR SORROWS
1996

"How about *'Drown your sorrows in the blue lagoons of my eyes'*?" I fluttered my eyelashes at Maggie and Angelina so they would notice the lagoons. "Would that work? Or is it too daring?"

Angelina laughed. "That's really good, Helena! But you must also say something about yourself." She topped our glasses with Brunello di Montalcino.

"OK" I said. "How about *'Drown your sorrows in the blue lagoons of my eyes. A sophisticated European lady is looking for an adventurous and open-minded partner'*?"

"No, absolutely not," Maggie disapproved. "Too kinky. Try again!"

"You are right, no good. Well – how about *'Drown your sorrows'* etc and then *'A cultured European lady, slim 5'6", is looking for a kind-hearted, thoughtful man, 45-55, who loves to be alive'*?"

We looked at each other, thumbs went up. "Quick!" I said, "Let me write it down before I forget. I'll send it off as soon as I get back to London, I promise." We chinked our glasses. "Who is next?"

Last year, the three of us had passed the 50th birthday milestone and the present trip to Tuscany was our treat. We were staying in Montalcino: sight- seeing, wine-tasting, eating and talking. This was Angelina's home town. She blossomed in her home territory. In London she presented herself as an exotic tigress, but here she was one of the many Italian mammas, warm, chatty and hedonistic, with a full figure and dark unruly hair over her shoulders. Quite a contrast to Maggie who always championed a strictly classical elegance, neat and trim, and to me - an eternal

133

tramp with comfortable walking shoes and a touch of a middle aged hippie.

We had met as students in London at King's College some thirty years ago and kept in touch all these long years. When we met we were all married, now we are all divorced. The children came to all of us at about the same time. 'There must be a virus going round!' people at the college teased us.

The years of coupledom were busy: coping with work, childminders, dining at each other's houses, sometimes even holidaying together. And then the divorces. It just happened that again the three of us went through them at the same time although by then we were already working at different places. Maggie's husband was sure I started it, stirred things up, but that wasn't true.

It took a long time before we were able to talk openly about our marriages but once we started we found we were a great help to each other. We called ourselves a 'Consciousness Raising Group', a CRG. Such groups were all the rage then, in the eighties, and it was Maggie's idea to call us that. Maggie was an American and had least constraints about talking private matters. She would just phone and say "Can we have another CRG session please? I need one badly!"

No more dinners, but CRGs. Perhaps the talking speeded things up, but it didn't stir them up. The three of us, each in our own way, were already, little by little, progressing towards the bitter ends of our marriages. The talking may have made that progress faster than it would have been otherwise - had our thoughts gone round and round and round only in our own befuddled heads.

Now that we were facing our sixth decade, with our academic careers painstakingly established and with the children grown up, wouldn't it be nice if........Well, we had decided that during this trip, while basking in Tuscany's sun full of pasta and pecorino, relaxed and affable, we would compose an advert each and send it off to a broadsheet paper of our choice. I am talking nineties here; online dating was only just beginning.

Maggie, the sensible one, was initially against the idea.

"Waste of time and too dangerous. Most of the replies will surely be from married men looking for something on the side. And the rest of them will be from some hopeless cases that I could just gobble up for breakfast."

Maggie's life seemed always to be in check. She didn't mess around; focused and practical she managed one task after another. Her goals were clearly stated. Not that she wouldn't occasionally give in to her desires, but she managed to keep her distance, her expectations well grounded in the real world, well under control.

"There will be no miracles, you have to remember that," she said. "How can we know who they really are? They can tell us anything they like!"

"Body language." Angelina said. She was the one with most experience.

"Of course you'd meet them at a public place at first. You'll talk, you'll watch, you'll soon know." Angelina had already placed several such adverts and seemed to have fun. Men entered her life and left again, sometimes they came back. Even her ex-husband re-appeared occasionally. Maggie and I were not quite sure what the nature of their relationship was. Angelina was like a battleship. Dressed up to the nines she sailed into parties surveying the terrain and gauging her chances. She didn't need to bother with adverts, but she liked to broaden her horizons. She loved to charm them all. Like a hunter she collected her trophies, often these were just the innocent pleasures of being admired.

"You know me, Helena. I don't ever want to live with a man again."

Angelina valued her freedom after enduring years of excessive jealousy from her controlling ex-husband.

"Don't take it so seriously, girls. You can't get everything you need from one man!"

Yet, Maggie and I could easily imagine her being a mamma, looking after her family, acting as a wonderful hostess, throwing dinner parties in her beautiful, immaculate home, entertaining people and radiating love and cheer. If she had enjoyed her singledom so much, why did she always worry about her daughter's lack of boyfriends? We didn't believe her; we imagined she would - if truth be told - have loved to be a domestic goddess.

Indeed - the three of us believed it would be very nice if we met someone. We all knew somebody who had met a Mr. Right through an advert so why not have a try? And what better place and time to mull over this than Tuscany in May? Perhaps the lagoons may catch the attention of an intelligent, kind, handsome, tall, curly-haired, sporty scientist or artist, or even a poet, who knows?

"Don't expect too much, Helena, take it easy!" Maggie stopped my musings. "We know what you are like!"

"Don't rush into anything silly, Helena!" Even Angelina thought it was necessary to warn me.

That was because I was a fool for love, always falling in and out of love, falling in with rose-tinted glasses on my nose and out once they fell off, usually within six months. Of course I knew angels don't exist, but I could magic them in by love and tolerance, by compassion and understanding, by curbing my criticisms. These emotional ups and downs were exhausting. I wished I could be less intense and keep my distance like Maggie or more easy-going like Angelina.

Waiting for a perfect man

"It's your turn now, Maggie" I said. We were looking at the extensive vineyards bathed in the glow of sunset. Behind us the ancient fortress, La Fortezza, was shining gold. It was mid May, the air was full of pungent scents and velvet-green hills were stippled with bright red poppies and yellow broom.

"Let's get it done with before dinner," Angelina smiled and, to encourage Maggie, she added: "I have booked a table at Villa del Fattore, highly recommended!"

"OK, here goes, "Maggie sighed. "But as I said, it's a waste of time."

She read out from her notes. *'An elegant and well travelled lady WLTM an intelligent caring man, 50s, with a GSOH'."*

"Add *'Come fly with me!'* at the beginning," I suggested. "It needs to be a bit sexier."

"Do I have to?" Maggie looked at Angelina feigning despair. "The longer the advert the more expensive."

"Oh yes, it needs a bit of spice! You are worth it, Maggie, remember!" Angelina confirmed my feeling. "How about: *'Come fly with me! An elegant and well travelled lady WLTM an intelligent caring man, 50s, with a GSOH'*.... and then...and then..." Angelina tried to remember the words. "And then add *'We'll just glide starry-eyed'.*"

"Excellent!" I started to sing. *'Come fly with me, let's fly, let's fly away, if you could use some exotic booze'....*" Again we chinked our glasses. "We'll just glide starry-eyed! That's good! Just do it, Maggie!"

We felt we were definitely making progress.

"Well, I'll be damned if anyone worth looking at answers such hogwash!" Maggie pointed her forefinger at us. "I'll blame you for any shambles that may come out of this."

Angelina hugged her. "You'll be grateful to us! And now it's my turn.....and afterwards..." She smacked her lips in anticipation. "Afterwards I am going to order ribollita followed by some delicious fish."

Angelina opened her notebook. "I have done my homework, what do you think of this? *'A fabulous Italian woman in her prime, loves art, music, cooking, socialising, seeks a confident, accomplished and positive man, 40s or 50s, must be over 5'10" and caring'.*" Angelina knew what she deserved. Maggie and I agreed there was nothing to be added, nothing to be changed. We called for a taxi to take us down to the renowned Villa del Fattore by the Orcia River.

The dream-like beauty of the landscape silenced us; we sat in the car absorbed in our own thoughts, observing the radiant hills with vineyards and sturdy farmhouses surrounded by cypress trees. Later on, once we had got over the excitement of choosing the food and admiring the Villa, Angelina returned to the topic of the day with a hint of melancholy in her voice. "My daughter should be doing this, not me."

"She'll find somebody in due course, give her time," Maggie, the sensible one, comforted her. "I think my son would be delighted if there was a new man by my side. It would take the weight off his shoulders. Who wants to be saddled with a single mum?" She couldn't help herself and added "Anyhow, aren't *you* happy to be single and free? So why should your young daughter rush into commitments?"

"She is not that young any more, she'll be 28 this summer." What worried Angelina most was her daughter's immersion in work to the exclusion of any socialising. "The biological clock is ticking, isn't it? I'll never be a grandma at this rate!" She twisted her glass this way and that. In spite of her momentary blues, she relished the garnet colour of her wine and its earthy aroma.

"She's got plenty of time," Maggie said. "Women often wait until their forties nowadays."

"Forties! Mamma mia! My Mum became a granny at forty!"

"If my sons knew what I was doing...." I joined in to add to the gloom. "If my sons knew that I am trying to sell myself in the Guardian, they would be so awfully embarrassed they would deny any acquaintance. Still..... I agree with Maggie, I also think both of them would be greatly relieved if a partner appeared on the scene. Sometimes I almost feel I'm trying so hard because of them, to lighten their load." Maggie nodded her head sympathetically.

Angelina smiled and sipped her wine. Encouraged, I continued. "I won't tell them about my disasters any more. No point to raise their hopes and cause further embarrassment."

Angelina raised her glass. "Let's drown our sorrows in style. This Brunello is just perfect!"

At that moment the chef, the capocuoco, arrived to inquire if everything was all right. Were we happy? And it was. We were.

LOW FAT DIET

1998

After a day of dreary work Sandra collapsed in front of the telly and, as usual, soon fell asleep. Sometime later she woke up with a start.

"Where am I? What time is it?"

Under dishevelled hair, her hazel eyes stared drowsily around. The telly still flickered, but the screen was empty. All was dark and quiet, except for Snoopy snoring in his basket. Slowly Sandra got up and went upstairs to her bedroom. Her thoughts flickered, jumping from one pending task to another, wandering from one worry to the next, as if the TV channels still flipped in her head. She curled up under the blanket and waited until weariness took hold of her again.

Early in the morning Sandra was woken by noise next door. Richard was getting up. She put on her nightgown and went to the kitchen to prepare her husband's breakfast. It was her morning routine: bacon and eggs, buttered toast and a strong coffee. She didn't approve of his eating habits but that's what he liked. His mood always improved after a good meal. And all she wanted now was peace, no arguments anymore.

"Breakfast's on the table!" she shouted.

"It's gonna be a hard day today," Richard said as he entered the kitchen taking the last drag from his cigarette. His belly was covered by a pristine light blue shirt and a grey blazer with a subtle blue check. White thick hair and sideburns were carefully cut. Above a matching tie, his round puffy face stayed impassive as he added "Good morning!" to greet his wife. He settled down to his breakfast, munching and browsing through some magazines.

141

"Some more coffee?" Sandra asked.

"Thanks." He drank it quickly. "Back at about seven," he said and off he went.

"Have a nice day," Sandra murmured at the closing door.

After he left, she took the dog out for a walk. Snoopy, a salt-and-pepper mini Schnauzer, barked excitedly. His long white beard and white eyebrows made him look like a funny old man.

"Come on, Snoopy sweetheart, what a lovely day! Who's a lucky boy today? Who's going to get a delicious breakfast?"

Talking to him continually, Sandra walked their customary round of suburban streets and then coaxed him back home.

"Here you are Snoopy Doopy." She gave him his breakfast. "Are you going to miss your mistress? Of course you are!"

Today, Sandra was to lead yet another workshop on stress management for a group of business directors. Not very exciting, but the socialising was fun. At least it used to be.

"Oh God!" she sighed staring at herself in the mirror.

She was a short, stocky woman in her late fifties. Her hair used to be chestnut brown, but now she preferred a lighter tone; less contrast with her pale skin. Her style was conservative, colours subdued, shoes sensible, makeup minimal. She liked to keep herself fit, recently she had joined a hiking club. With a bit of care, she was still a good looking woman.

"I'll be back soon, sweetie pie, don't be sad." She pushed the little schnauzer out of her way and left.

Snoopy, the mini Schnauzer

Richard's drive to the hospital was not a pleasant one. Congested traffic, adrenalin and dark thoughts. Nobody seemed to appreciate his efforts. Sandra was inattentive and the children hardly found time to visit anymore. And when they came, they were not interested in his stories. Too macabre, they said. What do they know about lives hanging on a thread, hearts that won't start beating? Can they imagine life-and-death decisions that he has to make daily? Such thoughts upset him and his blotchy face got redder. If only he could have a bit more understanding at home. He calmed himself down with another cigarette. As he began to think about the day's schedule, his small grey eyes behind frameless glasses brightened up. He loved his work. A valve replacement was on his list today and Richard was excited about the complicated and risky procedure of that operation. He smiled as he thought of his team. Always there for him, *they* never let him down.

Oh, and he must go and see how his old friend Johnny was doing. He had a triple bypass yesterday, a badly needed one. Amazing how long Johnny had lasted with that clogged coronary of his! He was always such a robust man, his ischemia was a

143

surprise. They went to the same university and used to play tennis together – that was a long time ago. All went well though and today Johnny will need some guidance and comforting. He entered the hospital with a satisfying feeling of being needed.

"Good morning everyone!"

Richard was an expert in his field, the most popular consultant cardiologist.

Sandra, a stress management consultant, was wearing a beige suit with a light pink scarf around her neck for a bit of colour. She had covered all the bullet points on developing specific strategies for conflict resolution. The eyes of the small company directors were fixed on various examples of stress anticipation. Most of these directors were sent here by their management boards to improve their interpersonal skills without expecting that it would make any difference. Both Sandra and the directors knew that it was just something to be ticked off on their CVs. So everyone was happy to hear the tea trolley approaching at last.

"Let's have a break now," Sandra beamed, "and after that we'll discuss your own experiences of stress management."

That was the part they all enjoyed best. She let them talk while her mind raced towards the shopping to be done and the overcrowded buses to be endured. She decided on a roast chicken dinner tonight; Richard will be pleased with that.

After a successful operation, Richard had enjoyed a cigarette before he finally found some time to stroll to the ward where his friend was recovering.

"How are you feeling, old chap? You will pass your MOT this time, I am sure!"

"Thank you, Richard," Johnny stretched his arms towards him. His pale face almost blended with the sheets that covered his long body. Only his black intense eyes, now filling with tears, were clearly visible.

"I feel so much better!" he said. "Soon I'll be playing tennis again. You are a magician!"

"Now now, Johnny," Richard put his hand on the patient's shoulder. "Take it easy. Mild exercise to start with, gradually increasing in intensity. Low fat, high fibre, no smoking, alcohol down to one or two units per day, you know the rules, don't you?"

"You're one to talk, Richard!"

"Well, it's you, not me, who wants to live to a ripe old age, isn't it?" Richard gave Johnny a big hug and left.

"My knee hurts" Sandra said as she sat down for dinner.

"It's bound to get worse, we're not getting any younger." Richard shrugged his shoulders and tucked into the chicken roast.

Sandra watched him. "Is the meat tender?" she asked for reassurance.

"Yes, it's good." He nodded.

"I thought you'd like a roast tonight."

"I've had a hard day." His tone became insistent. "Six hours on my feet. And then I had to rush off to a useless meeting with a new pushy director."

"Really?" Sandra was gently scratching Snoopy's head. "And how did Johnny's valve replacement go today?"

"It was a triple bypass and it was yesterday." Richard looked heavenwards.

"Sorry, I'm getting it all mixed up." Sandra was filling Richard's plate with a second helping. "My stress workshop went really well today," she said.

The rest of the dinner passed in silence, interrupted only by a few sweet nothings directed at Snoopy.

Later on there was a phone call from their daughter Luisa.

"How are you? Everything all right with the flat? ...How much?... No!" Richard's smile froze. "Well ......Mum wants to have a word."

"How is the new flat?" Sandra inquired. "Do you need anything? ...And when shall we see you?......I see.....All right then, bye."

Back at the table, Richard and Sandra exchanged looks of resignation.

"Luisa spends half her miserable salary on that bloody flat!" Richard muttered.

"And we've got so much space here!" sighed Sandra.

She loaded the dishwasher and settled down in front of the telly, cuddling Snoopy.

Richard took a sip of whisky, lit a cigarette, inhaled, exhaled and watched the smoke forming patterns in the air. After a while he turned towards the TV set in front of which his wife was fast asleep.

'No chance of any conversation here' he thought, flipping from one channel to another.

Finally the telly, the whisky and the smoke had their desired effect and he was ready for bed. Avoiding any more glimpses of his sleeping wife, he got up and climbed the stairs, breathing heavily.

"Where am I, what time is it?" Sandra woke up with a start.

The room was dark. Snoopy snored in his basket and the telly flickered in the corner. In the silence of the house, she could feel and even hear palpitations of her own heart. She felt shaky and tense. Forlorn, drowsy and dazed, she stared at the empty glimmering screen, when suddenly it came to life! A tall, handsome man appeared. He was in his late fifties or so, but well preserved, rucksack on his back, solid boots on his feet. Obviously an experienced hiker. He stepped out from the screen.

"Sandra, would you like to join me for a fortnight hike in Stubai Alps?" His lean, mature, weathered face radiated calm, kindness and fun.

"Who are you? Why me? I am not ready!" she protested.

"Edward, Ed, remember me? We met at the walkers' club." He smiled. "You kept me company when coming down Blumentahl Valley last summer, remember?"

"Oh yes, Ed..... Blumentahl Valley..... That was nice!" She did remember.

"Wasn't it?" Edward employed a serious, pleading look. "To be honest, Sandra, I have booked for two and was let down. The place is yours if you want it and if you can act now. Do come!"

Sandra's panic and bewilderment rapidly changed into pure exuberance. "Well...perhaps..."

"Have you got good boots and waterproofs? They can go into my rucksack. You won't need much more. We should leave in an hour; I'll wait." Ed settled down in the armchair and leafed through a Stubai travel guide.

Sandra rummaged through her crammed wardrobe and gave him the boots, raincoat and over-trousers. A few personal things, including her best nightie, fitted into her small day sack. Quickly she ran into the kitchen to prepare Richard's breakfast: boiled eggs, three slices of buttered bread and a pile of sliced ham. She covered it with cling-film and wrote him a brief note. Edward's sinewy hand was pointing to his watch when she finally returned.

"I must be dreaming!" She giggled. The dawn was breaking already; it was time to go.

Richard rushed off to work in the morning and so he spotted Sandra's note only after he got back home at night:

'Dear Richard,

All of a sudden, I have had a holiday offer from the walkers club that I simply couldn't refuse. It came just when I am free of any workshops. I know I should have mentioned it at dinner, but I didn't dare, we were both tired and irritable. I hope you'll understand.

Everything is taken care of and I shall be back in two weeks' time. Miss Julie will look after Snoopy, she has got the key.

There is plenty of cooked food in the freezer, all you need to do is to take out a portion every morning and heat it up in the evening.

Pork goulash is on the top shelf.

The salami and goose liver from Johnny are on the second shelf.

Homemade burgers that you like so much are on the third shelf together with some sausages.

You can have chips or potatoes with the meat. Or, if you like, you'll find pasta and rice in the larder.

Chocolate cream cake at the bottom of the freezer is already cut into daily portions.

You have my mobile number - just in case.

Don't forget to take your pills after dinner!

Take care of yourself.

Yours Sandra.'

Somewhat puzzled at first, Richard soon settled down with pasta, goulash and a bottle of red wine. After dinner he opened a bottle of a Glenfiddich Liqueur, a present from his valve replacement patient. He smiled at the vision of two peaceful, undisturbed weeks ahead. He may invite the neighbours one evening, he thought. A nice couple, especially the wife, so bubbly and cheerful - and such a good listener.

A DAY IN THE LAB

2002

Rockefeller Building at 21 University Street – that's where I work. Below a grand portal with proud columns, arches and crests, there are four marble steps leading up towards a wood-panelled door. I enter and aim straight for the lift. When I feel energetic or when I want to lose weight, I mount the stairs to the fourth floor. Not today.

21 University Street

Simon is the first person I come across.

"Good morning Simon, how are you?"

"How should I know?"

"Are you well?"

"Not really. You never know..... one day you may just collapse....Why do you look at me like that?...... I don't care, it doesn't bother me."

"But I care."

"Do you?" Simon's bulging eyes are fixed on me. "Do you really?"

Professor Simon Cohen is a widower, a thin man of medium height with bushy grey eyebrows, bulging eyes and a hooked nose; he makes me think of Moses. His hair and beard are neatly cut, his shirt is clean and crisp. At 81, he still comes to the lab every day to do experiments, the results of which are unlikely ever to be written up. He doesn't care – he's got more than enough publications already.

"I enjoy it," he says. "What else should I do?"

On my way to the lab I have to pass Greg standing by the kettle. Greg doesn't say hello. He is a postdoc with Tobias in the lab next door to mine. Greg is permanently pissed off. He wears a scruffy T-shirt which displays the capitals 'FOAD' over his grandiose chest and beer belly. A protein that he had discovered also bears that name. Meaning Fuck Off And Die or the Factor Of Accelerated Demethylation as he readily explains to whoever dares to ask him. His round face is set into a permanent frown. Better to avoid him.

Plate reader

I enter my lab, eager to reach the Plate Reader and to check the results of yesterday's experiment. Just to think that only a couple of years ago we had to do these measurements manually – tube by tube! Technology is wonderful! It would have taken me half a day then - and now? The plate just goes in and comes out and hey presto – here they are!

Good results! Funny how I can get ecstatic just because secretion from mast cells went up! Or totally miserable when it didn't. Just because it fits with my hypothesis. It went as I expected, hoped for and desired, so all is well. Except that Nick, my postdoc, hasn't arrived yet – probably another late night with Greg. At least Marianne, my project student, is here, already setting up a new assay, busily pipetting samples into the wells. She is keen and intelligent; it's good to see her enthusiasm grow. I wonder what happened to Nick.

I am plotting the results, happy because my hunch had been right. The values fit together nicely, all except one – it must have been a mistake! Or perhaps not? We'll have to repeat the experiment. I am all aglow from thinking about the possible interpretations when Fiorella enters looking upset and miserable.

"Oh dear, is it something to do with your boss?"

"Yes, it's her again!"

Fiorella is Italian and works in a lab downstairs. She tries very hard to get on with her high-handed boss; sometimes she just needs to talk to calm down. We agree to have a chat in the afternoon, we'll meet for tea.

Oh my God! It's time for the tutorial.

"Are you OK, Marianne? Good, will be back in an hour."

When I come back from teaching, Nick is in the lab, late as usual, mumbling some apologies about his shower not working this morning. Marianne says she is sorry but she messed up the pipetting.

"Well never mind, it happens, let's start again, there are still some reagents left in the freezer."

Knock knock, it's Simon.

"Are you having lunch? Or are you frightfully busy and can't stop staring at those dreadful machines of yours?"

"In about 20 minutes? I just have to prepare some more cells with Marianne. Is it OK, Simon?"

"Anything you say."

"What have you got in there? Tomatoes? Ah, they are not what they used to be. In my home country, tomatoes were full of flavour!"

Originally Simon's Jewish family lived in Baghdad. They sat down and wept by the rivers of Babylon - as he says. Some 200 years ago, however, one of his ancestors, a carpet dealer, had an argument with an Ottoman clerk and the whole family relocated to Mumbai. Simon's father was sent to London to study medicine at University College; we are always reminded of that.

"He walked these very same corridors."

Simon never fails to mention this as we make our tortuous way to a departmental meeting or to a seminar or to the stores to fetch some chemicals or to the animal house. Simon's father wanted the same for his son so he sent him away from Mumbai, at the age of just 12, to a school in London.

"Wait a minute – it must have been 1933, or was it 1931? The worst thing that has ever happened to me."

Simon puckers his face when remembering the horror of it. He only went back to India once, just before the war, and never again after that. Still he calls India his home country.

"Listen to me!" Simon says. "Do what I say: go to Marks and Spencer's and buy those little cherry tomatoes. They taste better than those plastic ones. But you'll never do what I say."

"Simon, what will you do over the coming long weekend?"

"A long weekend? First time I have heard of it, how awful. Everyone is doing the same thing, everywhere is full of horrid people."

"You could visit your grandchildren or perhaps start writing your memoirs?"

"Whoever would like to read my memoirs? Damn the long weekend!" He kicks the wall angrily and walks off.

As I rinse my coffee mug and my lunch box, I am thinking that I'd certainly like to read Simon's memoirs. He told me about their spacious Mumbai house with a big garden filled with flowering plants and fruit trees. There was an aviary with colourful birds, he said. There were dogs and children running about - his two sisters and many friends. The family were looked after by a cook, a gardener, a Portuguese driver and many other servants who all lived there. Simon's mother, a sporty and beautiful lady, was the first woman to attend the University of Mumbai. His father was a doctor, respected and welcomed everywhere. That large house in his home country had apparently been pulled down; now a large block of flats stands there.

Nick had completed a session at the microscope and comes to show me the images. They are beautiful. Actin filaments glow majestically inside mast cells. I have seen them before but still get excited: before activation the filaments only line the cells' peripheral membranes, but in activated mast cells they suddenly fill the cellular universe, busily glimmering like fireflies, ready for action.

"When will you analyse the images?" I ask as equably as I can manage.

"I need to catch up with some older data first, but I think I can get started on these tomorrow."

"That would be good," I say. And pigs will fly I think to myself.

"They came out very well, didn't they?" Nick says proudly.

"Yes, they are brilliant." We smile at each other, sharing the wonder of it.

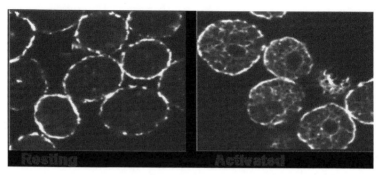

Actin filaments in resting and activated mast cells

Now I need to update my lecture for tomorrow. I open PowerPoint programme and stare at the images of neuromuscular junctions. *'At the end of this lecture students should understand.....'* I am searching the web for a sexy representation of voltage gated ion channels, adding an arrow here, question mark there. Suddenly Greg barges in.

"Have you got my 5 ml Eppendorf pipettor?"

"No."

"Someone took it."

"It wasn't me. Marianne? Nick? Have you seen Greg's Eppendorf?"

"No."

"Not me, mate." Nick salutes him and Greg barges out of the lab, cursing. It looks like he's got another bad day.

However, occasionally there are days when Greg is in a better mood, especially when he starts remembering the good old student times. What fun! They used to get legless at the Liverpool's Augustus John. He goes all misty-eyed. Drinking would be concluded with a good curry at the 'Liverpool Mumbai'. That was an excellent restaurant!

Greg is OK with blokes, but uneasy with women. In their presence, his frown changes into a questioning stare: what the hell do you think you are doing here? He feels better after he has quietly exchanged a few sneering asides with his boss Tobias. Better to avoid them both.

Next a phone call from my son Matthew. He will be coming home for the long weekend together with his brother Oliver. Great! I'll have to do some shopping tomorrow. A little more fiddling with the lecture, finally I save it on a memory stick and shut the computer down. Tea with Fiorella: we are discussing strategies for coping with her boss, calm, assertiveness, open mind. Meanwhile, Marianne has finished her work and is tidying up. The plates will be assayed tomorrow.

Knock knock.

"Am I disturbing you? I have come to say good night."

"Good night Simon, see you tomorrow."

"How do you know that? You never know.........but I very much hope so."

"All right Simon, God willing I'll see you tomorrow. Have a nice evening."

"Don't say that. Why should I? "

"Bye bye Simon!"

MY STUDY

2005

The bedrooms of Matthew and Oliver were always a mess, out of bounds. Once my sons left the nest, one of the bedrooms became my study. It changed its face very slowly and gradually so that only now I can call it my own.

One of its walls provides space for fitted wardrobes, light green with creamy white doors. That's where I hide *my* mess. Behind the creamy white, piles of notes and documents are organised and re-organised without much success. I move papers from one file to another and keep changing the folders' names. The 'Muscle Lectures' file was re-named 'State Pension' and the 'Cell Cycle' changed into a 'Last Will' folder. The 'Children's Drawings' file stayed as it was, although some of its contents were reluctantly discarded. The old 'Travel' file had changed into 'Superannuation', but the new 'Travel Section' continues to grow and comprises numerous sub-categories. The two largest files are called 'Various 1' and 'Various 2'. I'll have to sort them out one day.

A large square cloth occupies most of the wall at a right angle to the wardrobes. It displays a print of the front of a huge truck, evoking 1940s. 'Boom! Boom!' it says on both sides of the truck's grill, just underneath the windscreen wipers. The front lights glow as the red and brown relic whizzes through a matching brown frame.

The boys loved the truck when they were little, but it soon got replaced with flamboyant posters of Prince, idol of Matthew, and Robert Plant of Led Zeppelin fame, Oliver's hero. I had rediscovered the truck print in the loft during the Big Clearout and

157

washed away the dust and stains as well as I could. Now I love to watch it hurtling towards me as I write.

Boom! Boom!

Opposite the wardrobes is a small grey sofa that can be opened up to serve as a double bed for visitors. Above the sofa is a large square painting by a very grumpy friend of mine. It shows a black wall with a black, white-framed, window that is slightly opened, just enough to let a ray of greenish light in, gloom and hope combined. It has a simple golden frame made by another friend; he wasn't grumpy at all but liked his drink too much. Next to the painting hangs a cork board. After my travels, I stick postcards on it showing paintings from newly discovered museums and galleries.

Below the cork board and the postcards is my desk, the top of which used to serve as a breakfast bar. That was in the last century, in the kitchen of another house, in my previous life that doesn't seem to be part of me anymore. Now the desktop is supported by four small drawer units of a cheap DIY variety, stained mahogany. They are full of pencils and papers, incomprehensible computer and printer instructions and accessories. Black Laptop sits proudly on the top of the desk.

"I have all the answers," it promises. "Ask me anything!"

We have an intense love-hate relationship.

My latest acquisition is an office swivel chair from Ikea – it's black, matching both the grumpy friend's painting and the laptop. I think I look good sitting on it in my black outfit, drinking tea, writing and surfing the net, but I have to go now and get some exercise.

I'll be back soon.

A CHRISTMAS TREAT

2008

"You must do it, Helena!" Julie exclaimed as she tucked into her grated carrots.

We'd just finished our weekly swim at the Surbiton Gym and, as usual, followed it at the Health Bar by a few salads and a bit of gossip. We didn't have much time since Christmas was looming ahead, but still - Julie was determined to twist my arm.

"You'll find Vladimir just wonderful!" she raved. "He's an excellent masseur and what's more – his looks are heavenly!" Julie's eyes twinkled, she pouted her lips sensuously as she popped a morsel of tofu into her mouth. "Tall, muscular, blond. And his eyes are amazing steely blue."

"Hmm, it does sound good..." I weakened. "I've never had a massage before - I suppose it could be my Christmas Treat."

"He's very popular, you know." Julie smiled and winked. "You better book yourself soon or...."

"Don't overdo it, Julie!" I cut her short. "Keep some of the thrill for your husband."

That was nasty of me. I knew Julie and Robert hadn't shared a bedroom for some years. She remained silent while we shared a courgette and lentils salad.

"How is it going with Jonathan?" She reciprocated after a while.

"Hmm, not too well," I squirmed. "Not sure which way it's going....it's up and down...I don't know, probably a dead end, but still - I keep trying."

Wink, wink, again when we parted. Julie just couldn't help it. "Merry Christmas! See you in two weeks, Helena! Book right NOW, tonight!" As we embraced, she pushed Vladimir's card into my hand.

160

I phoned him as soon as I got home. 'If not now, when?' I told myself.

"You are lucky," his husky voice answered, "there is just one last slot before Christmas."

"Good," I said, "and I want a full hour please; whole body massage, I deserve it!" I didn't need to say that. Words just came out of my mouth.

"I am sure you do." His voice sounded smooth and velvety now.

After this exchange, I poured myself a shot of whisky and sat down on the sofa. I imagined Vladimir's steely blue eyes staring at my ageing body and felt nauseous.

Two days later, I climbed the stairs to reach the 'Sports Injury Clinic' situated just above our Surbiton Gym. I wasn't looking forward to meeting Vladimir at all. I was tired and apprehensive; not ready to face Vladimir's stare. It felt more like a punishment than a Christmas Treat. Why did I allow Julie to get me into this mess? I rang the door-bell and a tall, blond guy appeared in all his glory, just as Julie described him. He wore white cotton trousers and a white vest exposing his magnificent shoulders, over which a white towel was casually thrown.

"I.. I have an appointment," I mumbled.

"Please take a seat, ma'am. My colleague will be with you in a minute." Steely blue eyes stared through me vacantly.

A mixture of disappointment and relief swept over me. Soon, a young, wiry, very short guy entered into the foyer and beckoned me to follow him. Also dressed in white, but no revealing vest; his long-sleeved T-shirt had some flowery embroidery at the front and the Dharma wheel at the back. His dark eyes were friendly, but mischievous. Black, bushy, curly hair and a large

161

golden earring in the shape of a Celtic cross in his right ear completed the picture.

He led me to one of the small 'studios', a cubicle with a massage table in the middle.

"G-g-get yourself ready, m-ma'am," he stuttered and left the room discreetly.

To hell with Christmas, I thought as I looked around. There were shelves around the walls loaded with a multitude of bottles and stacks of neatly folded white towels. I grabbed the biggest one, stripped, wrapped the towel firmly round my torso and laid myself down carefully on a white sheet that covered the massage table. I stared at the ceiling. A cobweb in one corner and a few interesting cracks in another. Sweet aroma of lavender permeated the room, but it didn't sooth my tension. Just my luck! My Christmas Treat is a massage by a stuttering gnome.

Knock, knock. "Are you ready, m-madam?" The masseur entered gingerly. "My name is P-P-Peter. We'll start with your b-b-back. Would you turn around please?"

"I'm Helena," I managed a little smile. Clutching at my towel, I positioned myself onto my belly.

"L-lavender, r-rose or g-geranium?" Peter inquired.

"Lavender please."

"P-p-perfect. Excellent for relaxation. I'll add a touch of tea tree oil, Helena, it's g-good for beating winter colds. And off and off we go!"

He poured some of the oil mixture onto his hands and rubbed them together. I watched Peter's feet in white sandals through the nose-hole of the massage table. They were light and swift as if dancing. He began to sing.

"Heigh ho, heigh ho, it's off to work we go, heigh ho, heigh ho, heigh ho!" Peter lost his stutter when he sang. His hands radiated warmth and he was obviously enjoying himself. He worked away with ease and confidence.

"Stiff shoulders, Helena? V-very common." He continued to hum and occupied himself with the knots in my muscles. "Aha – here is a tough one!" he exclaimed, kneading away enthusiastically at a particularly tensed bit of my back. "It's not t-too rough, is it?"

"No, I like a good pummelling." I began to feel more at ease.

Lavender and Tea Tree Oil

"Are you looking forward to Christmas?" I ventured.

"Not all that much," his hands continued to glide over my back. "It's just lots of extra chores, isn't it?"

"Yes, quite stressful," I sighed, "we all worry about it, then eat too much and get fat."

"I'm not complaining." Peter chuckled. "I always have many c-customers after the season!"

"I'm going away to spend Christmas with my sister's family." I told him. "They are very friendly and hospitable and I think they like to have me around." I felt like confiding in him

although he was just a kid. "It's nice to be wanted, isn't it?........
Will you spend Christmas with your parents?"

"My f-father isn't alive anymore."

"Oh, sorry. Well, with your mother then?"

"No, I'll be with my f-flat-mate, we have started the
celebrations already."

"But getting presents is nice, isn't it?" I changed tack.
"Have you written to Santa yet?" Tingly warmth was spreading
over the right side of my back.

"Of c-course, I d-dropped a letter to him this m-morning.
Is it all right, Helena?"

"It's fine, absolutely fine. What did you wish for? Can you
tell me?"

"I wished for another joint of h-ham," said Peter, "My m-
mum gave me one as an early present, but we ate it already. In
just one sitting! M-me and my flat-mate. Mum will be cross."

His answer disarmed me totally.

"Where does it all go?" I wondered, my heart full of
empathy.

"That's what they all ask," he laughed. After a pause he
added: "and also f-for a g-girl-friend. Does it hurt, Helena?"

"No, it's really good. She'll come one day - when you least
expect it."

"I'm g-glad you like it.......I hope she will...... And
also....one d-day... I'd like to have my own s-studio." Peter sighed
wistfully.

"I'd recommend you to all my friends," I assured him.
"Your hands work magic!"

"Oh! Thanks!" Peter chuckled and then sighed again. "M-
mum will be with her b-boyfriend over Christmas and I don't like
him much. Anyhow, she'd be c-cross about that h-ham joint."

164

Peter started to work on the left side of my back. "Here we go again. Relax, Helena, you can s-sleep if you wish."

He started to sing again "In a mine, in a mine, in a mine, where a million diamonds shine."

"No, I don't want to sleep." I protested. "I want to enjoy it."

"That's nice to know." Peter's humming intensified as he continued the work on my back.

"I'd recommend your studio highly!" I repeated and began to drift off.

I closed my eyes and floated away, away from worries and confrontations, feeling safe and cared for. Someone else was in charge: Peter and his skilful hands. I let go. Yes, I must recommend Peter to my sister when she comes for a visit. Perhaps I can get some massage vouchers for my friends? I wondered whom I should send to Peter. How about Tobias who was the Head of our Department? That would be interesting.... I pictured Tobias stretched out on Peter's massage table. Full of himself as ever, he'd call to Peter: 'Press more on the left side, my boy!' And what would Peter do? He'd come up with some trick, for sure. He'd find his client's Achilles heel and make him groan. 'Is it ticklish, sir?' he'd ask innocently, adding more pressure onto the spot. 'Ouch, ouch!' Tobias would complain.

Stop it, what are you doing Helena? Think of someone nice......perhaps Jonathan? Would he like a voucher? No, no....too early....early days... It's no good to rush it....he'd get the wrong idea...just imagine....

'It's for you, Jonathan! A voucher!'

'A what?'

'A Caring Touch Christmas Voucher...See? ... Enjoy the Magical Power of Touch!.... Simple and Wonderful!'

165

'What are you talking about?'

'About a caring touch.'

'For goodness sake, forget it Helena.'

.......A caring touch... that would be a good name for Peter's studio....not very original though....lucky to have had Peter after all..... I must thank Julie, she can keep her Vladimir....

"And you? What about your wish Helena?" Peter's voice broke through my bliss. He had finished hacking my back and was kneading my calves now.

"Has your letter to Santa gone?" he inquired.

I turned my head to view his puckish face and grinned. "I wish Jonathan wasn't such a jerk! Never mind, my wish has been granted already. You are my present from Santa, my Christmas Treat!"

"Your wish is my command!" Peter performed an elaborate bow. "Happy to be of service."

His stutter seemed to have disappeared alongside with my tension. His warm hands fluttered around me. One last long stroke and then he laid his palms quietly on my shoulder blades to indicate that's it, the end.

"Well – thank you, that was fantastic!"

"I'll see you outside when you are ready," he left the room with a wink.

Dressed and feeling young and beautiful, I came out to find Peter sitting behind the reception desk next to Vladimir. Not in white anymore, he wore a black baggy woolly jumper with a large smiling head of Rudolph the Red Nose Reindeer on his chest. Vladimir was still in white cottons, steely eyes above his stupendous chest staring into space.

"Hello there Vladimir," I greeted him without fear. "Merry Christmas!"

Startled, he focused his gaze on me with moderate interest and gave a little mechanical smile. I waved my hand at him and turned to Peter to pay my bill.

"Thanks again, Peter, you made my day." I gave him a generous tip and wished him a Happy New Year.

"I'll be back," I said, "perhaps in your new studio? And I'm sure to send you new customers too. Do you do massage vouchers?"

"Not yet, but I could do, a good idea!" he said and gave me a peck on the cheek.

As usual after festive season indulgencies, our first session at the Surbiton Gym was a tough one. Moaning and groaning and exchanging details of our new diets, we worked extra hard. But as soon as Julie and I arrived at the Health Bar and settled down, Julie asked the inevitable question.

"Well? How was it?" Her mouth was stuffed with roasted buckwheat groats and she splattered them around. Undeterred, she waved her fork in front of my face. "Would you like to taste some of this?"

"No thanks, I'll stick to beetroot juice today. Actually - I didn't see Vladimir in the end."

"Oh silly you! I'll just have to drag you there one day.....I won't give up."

"No, no, I did go. But I saw Peter, not Vladimir. I mean I had a glimpse of Vladimir, but Peter was my masseur."

"Peter?" Julie's face was full of concern. "That little chap who stutters? I've seen him around."

"He was absolutely brilliant. Julie, you got me onto a good thing, thank you! When I can afford it, I'll go again."

167

I finished the juice and helped myself to some of Julie's buckwheat after all - I was starving.

"This Vladimir of yours – why do you like him?" I asked her. "He seemed a bit... distracted."

Julie pushed the remaining groats around her plate.

"He doesn't say much, true. Sometimes he talks about body building, gives me exercise suggestions. That suits me fine. I just flop down, unwind, and enjoy the only bodily contact I get these days."

"But Julie, can't you do something about Robert?"

"No, I can't." She shook her head.

"And how is it going with Jonathan?" she inquired full of feigned concern.

I got up to get another salad.

"Did you have a nice and cosy Christmassy time together?" Julie insisted.

"No, not really. You know I can't do much about Jonathan either."

"Why the hell not?" Julie's concern was for real now.

"We don't have much in common. All he wants is for me to adjust to his routines. I try and try but there is a limit, isn't there?"

"Well, Helena," she said as we embraced, "same time next week?"

"Sure, Julie, I'll be here. We must keep up the good work."

"It was a lovely service." Diana smiled at Bob's sister. "The Queen's 'Bicycle Race' song was a very good choice. It's so good to have finally met you, Margaret. I only wish it were at a happier occasion."

"Bob was very fond of you, Diana. He talked about you a lot. It's good that you have stayed in touch with him in spite of everything." Margaret and Diana embraced.

"This is Tim, my husband," Margaret said.

"Nice to meet you, Diana, shame about the circumstances." Tim offered a plate of spring rolls. "Have you seen the collection of Bob's photographs yet?" he asked Diana. "Margaret had a good rummage around to find them. I believe you have sent some too?"

"Yes, I have. They were from our cycling holidays. Forty years ago! My God!" Diana counted on her fingers to make sure. "Forty two, I can't believe it."

"There were quite a few surprises for us with these photos," Tim said. "So many friends! So many ladies! We never knew that side of Bob's life."

"No, we only knew him in the family circle." Margaret said. "Our daughter Stephie loved his visits! She always had fun with him. In summer he would lift her up to reach for the plums, he was so tall...or – in winter - he held her up so high she could pull down the icicles from the roof."

"Margaret used to get worried about all that romping. Didn't you, Margaret?" Tim put his arm around his wife's shoulders. "Stephie, come and say hello to Diana!"

"Uncle Bob was always fun," Stephie said as she shook hands with Diana. "He could be really entertaining. Sometimes a little too much." She looked at her parents. "I couldn't recognize him in these old photos, so slim and fit-looking, how could he have changed so much?"

"Well, Bob always did exactly what he wanted, he was stubborn," Tim said. "He knew how to enjoy himself...."

"He always came home for Christmas, always," Margaret interrupted. "Except the last two years – he was too unwell."

"Bob was a generous, witty and charming man, incredibly strong," Diana put in quickly. That's how she wanted to remember him. "A very sociable man, big-hearted. We had some good times together. But I couldn't save him from himself.....no one could.... it was hard. Still, we remained friends even after we had split up."

The board with Bob's photos was surrounded by people. Ex-girlfriends, neighbours, walkers, cyclists, socialisers.

"Is that really him? I can't believe it."

"Wasn't he a good looking man when young?"

"Who is this woman? Is that a wedding photo? I didn't know Bob was married."

"To Brenda, but only for a short time. She cheated on him. He wouldn't put up with any silly business, would he?"

"Where was she from?"

"Some exotic place, Seychelles I think."

"They looked good together."

Yes, they did, Diana had to admit. Young Bob, tall, slim and handsome, looking like an Oxford graduate in his round black-rimmed glasses, embracing his exotic dark-skinned bride. Diana met Bob some four years later, when Brenda was already gone and Bob almost, but not quite, recovered from her betrayal. By that time he looked more like a cross between Tom Selleck and Zorba the Greek. Unpretentious, down-to-earth, towering over her like a knight in shining armour. It made her feel safe and protected. Yes, to start with they had a great time together. Bob was constantly planning endless escapades but he was also ready to help her whenever she needed him. A couple of drinks made him even more amusing, at least initially. He was hilarious and irresistible. Bob's humour and lack of ostentation put everyone at ease. There was a dark side to him though, spreading quietly like a slow poison. He was too strong to notice, denying any problems and getting away with it for a very long time. Diana's protests made no difference. Everybody here knows.

Diana browsed through the photos.

"Look! That's me!" She pointed one out to a slim lady in a bright red dress that was standing right next to her.

"No!"

"Yes it is, definitely. It was forty two years ago. We were camping in Portugal."

"What a lovely photo!" The lady introduced herself. "I'm Susanne, one of Bob's cycling friends."

"Nice to meet you, Susanne," Diana said. "I only wish it were at a happier occasion."

"Yes, what a shame."

"We were actually cycling in Portugal – can you see the bikes just there, showing behind the tent?"

"That must be Bob's old bike." Susanne commented. "Just before he got ill, he acquired this most amazing expensive super bike. He only used it a couple of times. I wonder what happened to that bike."

Diana would have so much liked to tell Susanne more about the Portuguese holidays with Bob, but Susanne's attention was gone.

"Oh – excuse me, I must say hello to George." Susanne fluttered off to place a juicy kiss on the cheek of an elderly bold man in a black suit.

"George! Hello! I haven't seen you for ages."

"Susanne! How are you? Don't you look well!"

"Thank you, George. I am the only one here who is wearing some colour! I thought Bob would approve."

"I am sure he would," George said. "You were also the only one to whose bollocking he'd listen."

"Yes, he liked to listen all right, but he carried on, didn't he? The bollocking amused him, that's all. And you, George, how are you? Are you still with Maisie?"

"Oh yes, we are married now. Ten years already."

"Goodness! I still remember when we first noticed there was something going on between you and Maisie. It seems like yesterday. Time flies!" Susanne sighed and straightened her red dress. "Well, we must soldier on," she said, ready to meet some more of the old pals. "Look, I can see Helena in front of Bob's photos, I should go and say hello to her."

"Susanne," George stopped her, "how is your love life, then?"

"Oh George, you know me, I'm still looking for the right person... Oh, isn't that Tony over there?"

"Wait, I have some other news for you: I am going to be a grandfather soon!"

"Congratulations, George!" Susanne kissed him again. "Is Katie expecting? Did she get married?"

"Yes, she is. She married a lawyer, a nice chap, I think they are ....."

"Wonderful!" Susanne exclaimed, waving her hand in Tony's direction. "George, can I introduce you to Diana? She knew Bob forty years ago – that's even longer than we did, amazing!" and she rushed off.

Diana and George commented on the sad circumstances of their meeting while they helped themselves to some more spring rolls from the trays on the counter.

"How did you know Bob?" George asked her.

"We used to go out together – years ago – we stayed in touch until the end."

"Shame about the end – but what else could one expect? With all that..."

"I know," Diana prevented him from saying any more, "but he was such a kind and generous person. A sort of gentle giant really, underneath all that."

"Yes, he was a very congenial man."

"Did you see the photos?" Diana pointed out the one from the Portuguese holidays. "You should see him cruising on his bike along the beaches of Praia de Mira, wind in his hair! He had plenty of hair then."

There was a ringing noise as, by now rosy-cheeked, Tim clinked his glass and raised it to propose a toast. Hotel staff started to fill everyone's glasses up with whisky. Tim thanked the guests for coming from afar to share the grief with the family and to remember and celebrate Bob's life. He talked about his unforgettable character.

"Let's drink to the memory of Bob, our gregarious brother, uncle and friend! Let's raise our glasses and toast with his favourite Oban whisky! We all know how fond he was of that stuff, he could consume a bottle without blinking."

Now Margaret touched Tim's sleeve and clinked her glass. "Please enjoy yourselves just as Bob would have liked you to."

Glasses were being filled again and conversation resumed with an increased vigour.

"The beaches were fantastic!" Diana continued. "We used to cycle during the daytime and went skinny dipping at night. Can you believe this is Bob?" She pointed out the photo again.

"It must have been hard for you, Diana, to see him change so much." George answered absentmindedly. He noticed that Helena was peering at the same photo.

"Hi, Helena, good to see you. Have you been on your bike lately? It's hard to find the time, isn't it? May I introduce Diana?"

After they had exchanged the usual pleasantries and discussed the joys of grand-parenting, Diana carried on with her Portuguese Cycling Story.

"We also visited Pinhão and went Port- tasting. Oh, you know, I think it was the best time of my life..."

Helena, as if from a great distance, watched both George's polite responses to Diana and the animated exchange between Tony and Susanne as the two of them were trying to remember the words of Queen's 'Bicycle Race' song.

Queen's Bicycle Race

Printed in Great Britain
by Amazon